Creative Stylized

Flower Patterns

For Those Who Like Designs Just That Little Bit Different

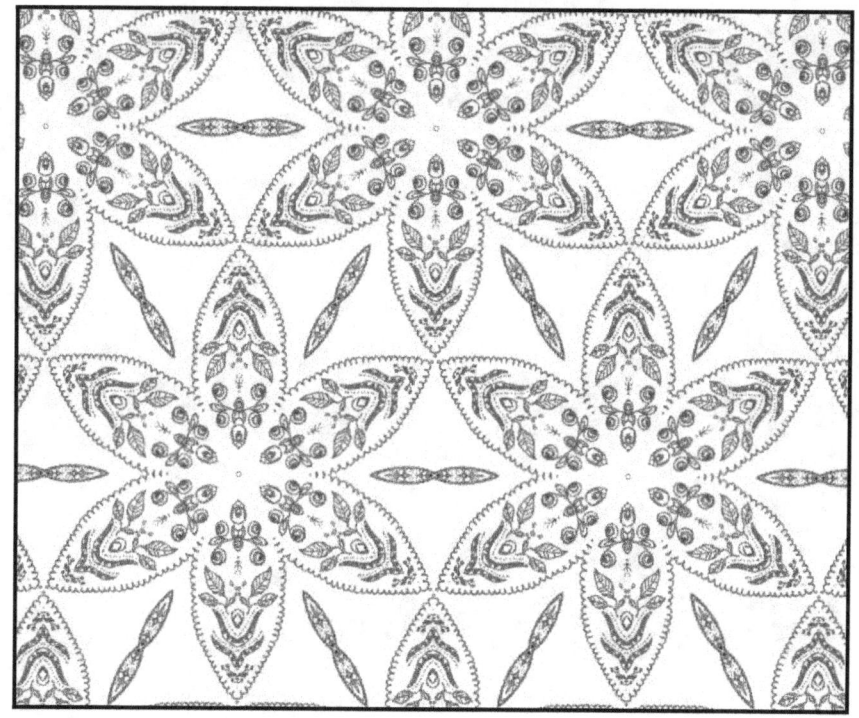

By: Kaye Dennan

KD Coloring Studio

ISNB: 978-1523418886

PUBLISHERS NOTES
Disclaimer

Paperback Edition

Manufactured in the United States of America

A note from the Illustrator

Creative Stylized Flower Patterns

This book was developed especially for those who like to work with interesting and often abstract designs.

The wide range of images in this book will give you the chance to extend your capacity for working with color and shapes.

These images will give you the opportunity to try out colors, shading and will keep you occupied for hours.

Did you know that colors affect your emotions?

Most of us have favorite colors and they are favorites because we like how they make us feel when we see them or even wear them.

Some people even find that their observance of a color a person is wearing affects the way that they initially react to a person: positively, negatively or cautiously. Basic relationships are listed below but the reality is that what might make one person feel cheerful can make another person feel irritated depending on the viewers' past experiences or cultural differences.

Warm Colors – Red, Orange, Yellow

Cool Colors – Green, Blue, Purple

Neutral Colors – Black, Gray, White, Tan, Brown

I encourage you to experiment with color and shapes and enjoy your coloring pass-time,

****

Every Second Page has been left blank so that you do not ruin one of your colored designs with color bleeding through the paper.

If you are using pencils then I would suggest you slide a piece of thin cardboard or thick paper under the page you are coloring just to prevent any pressure marks on the following page.

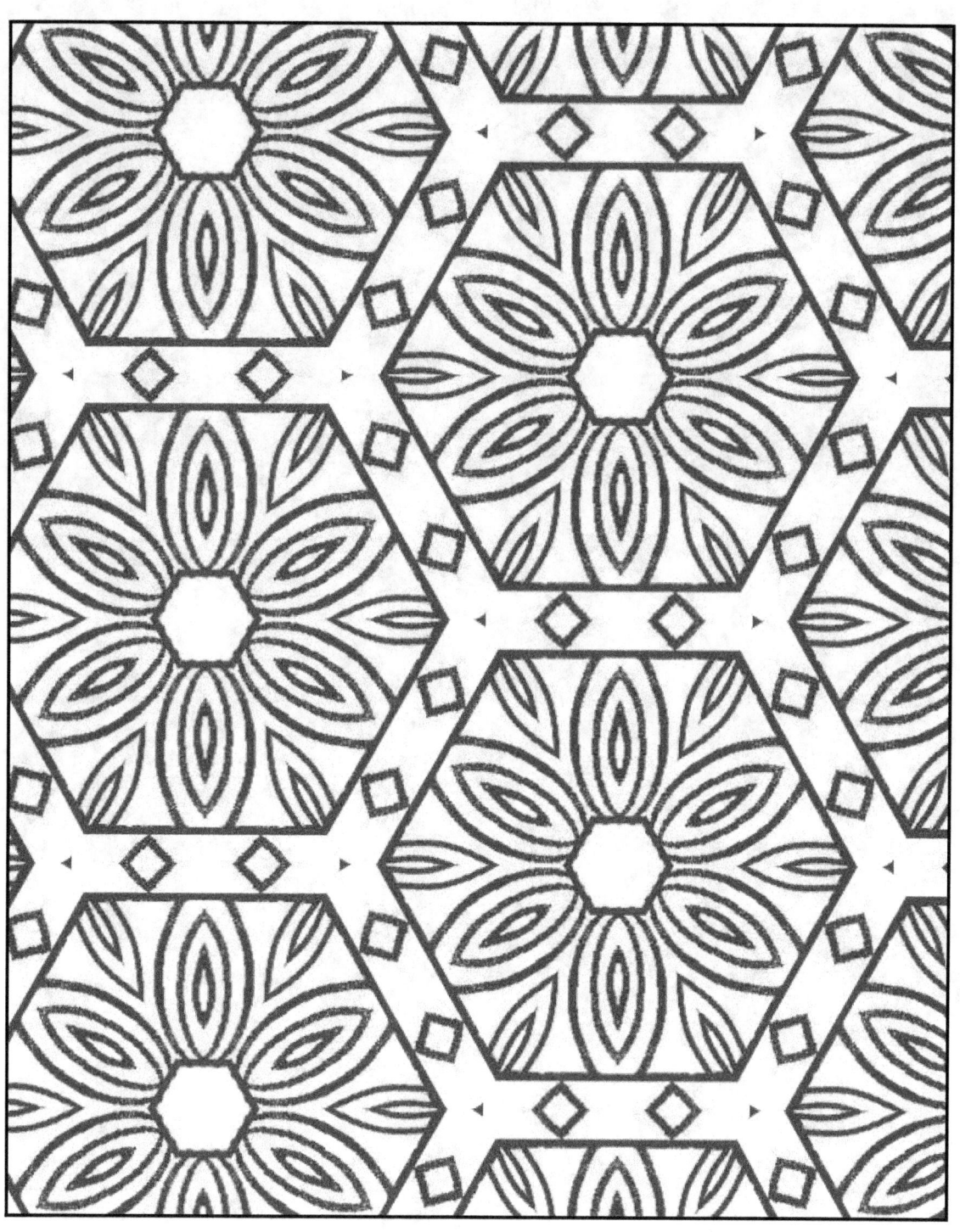

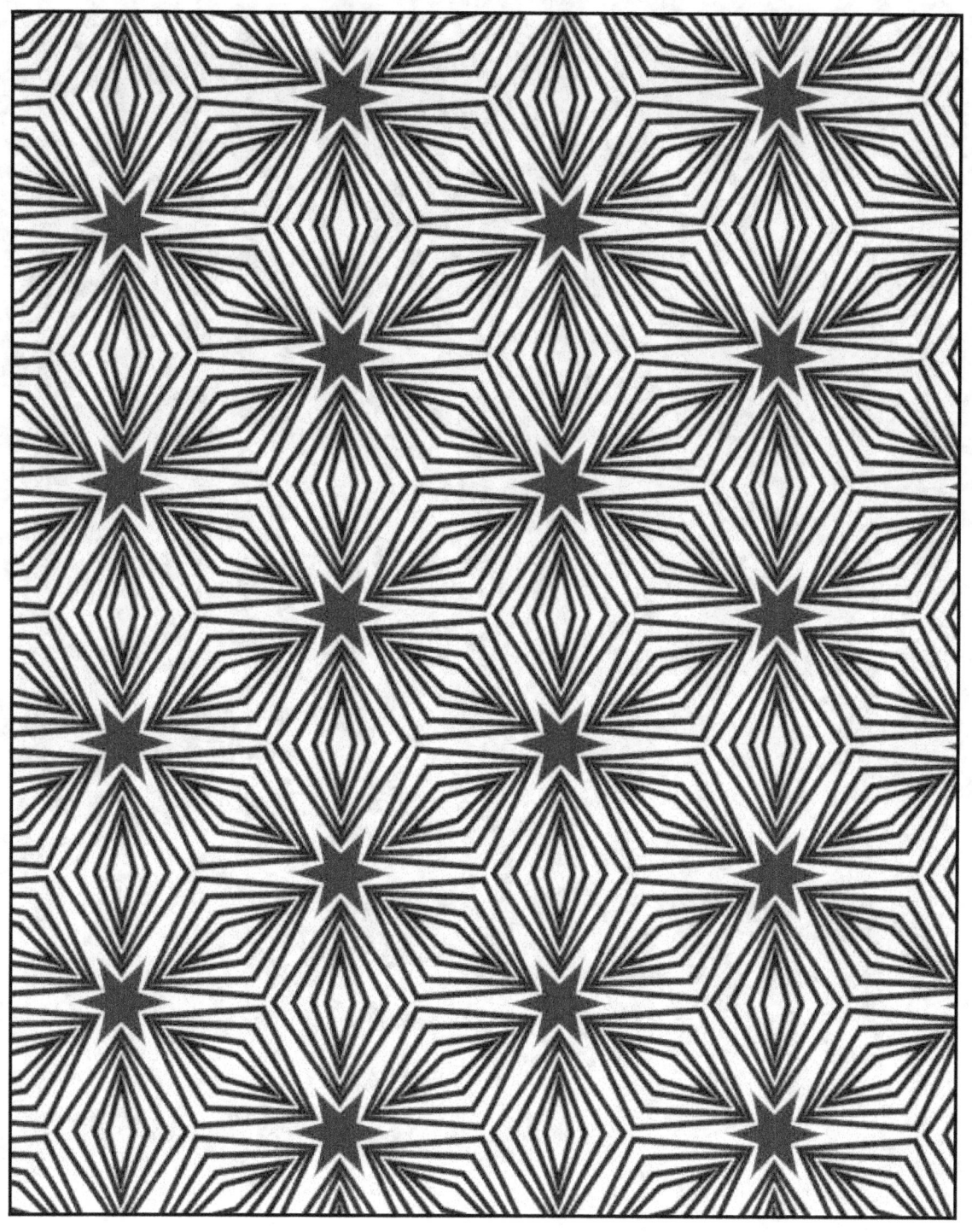

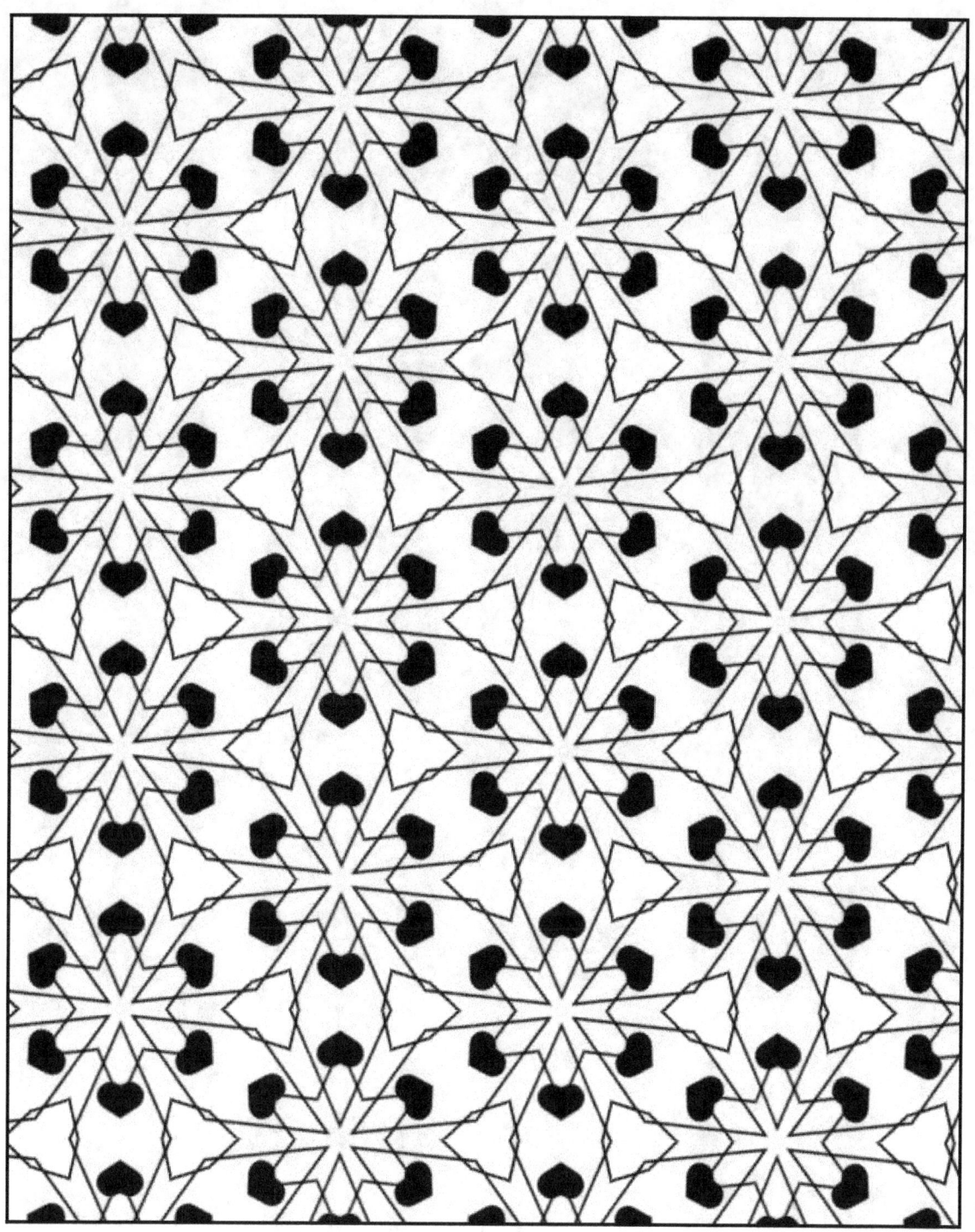

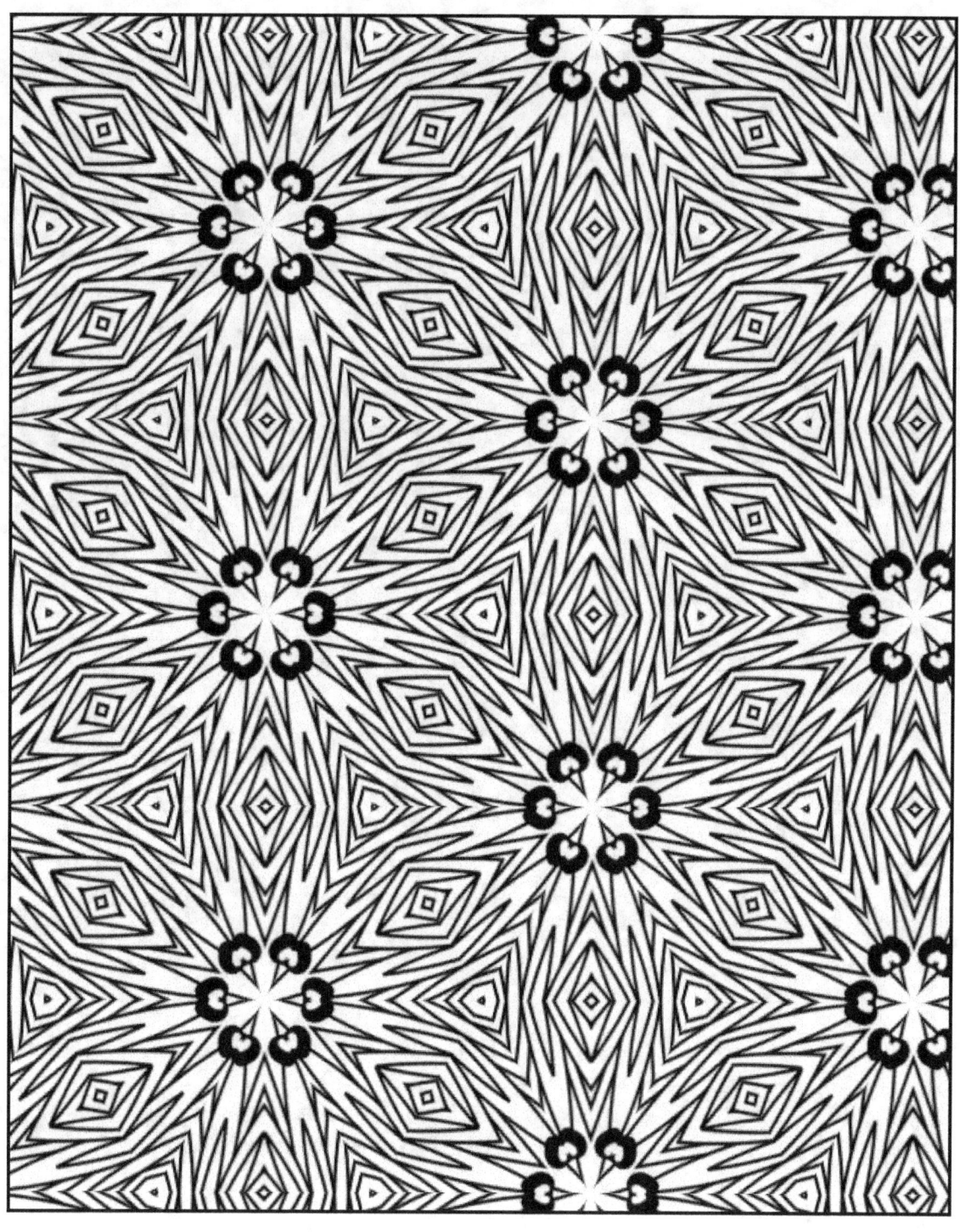

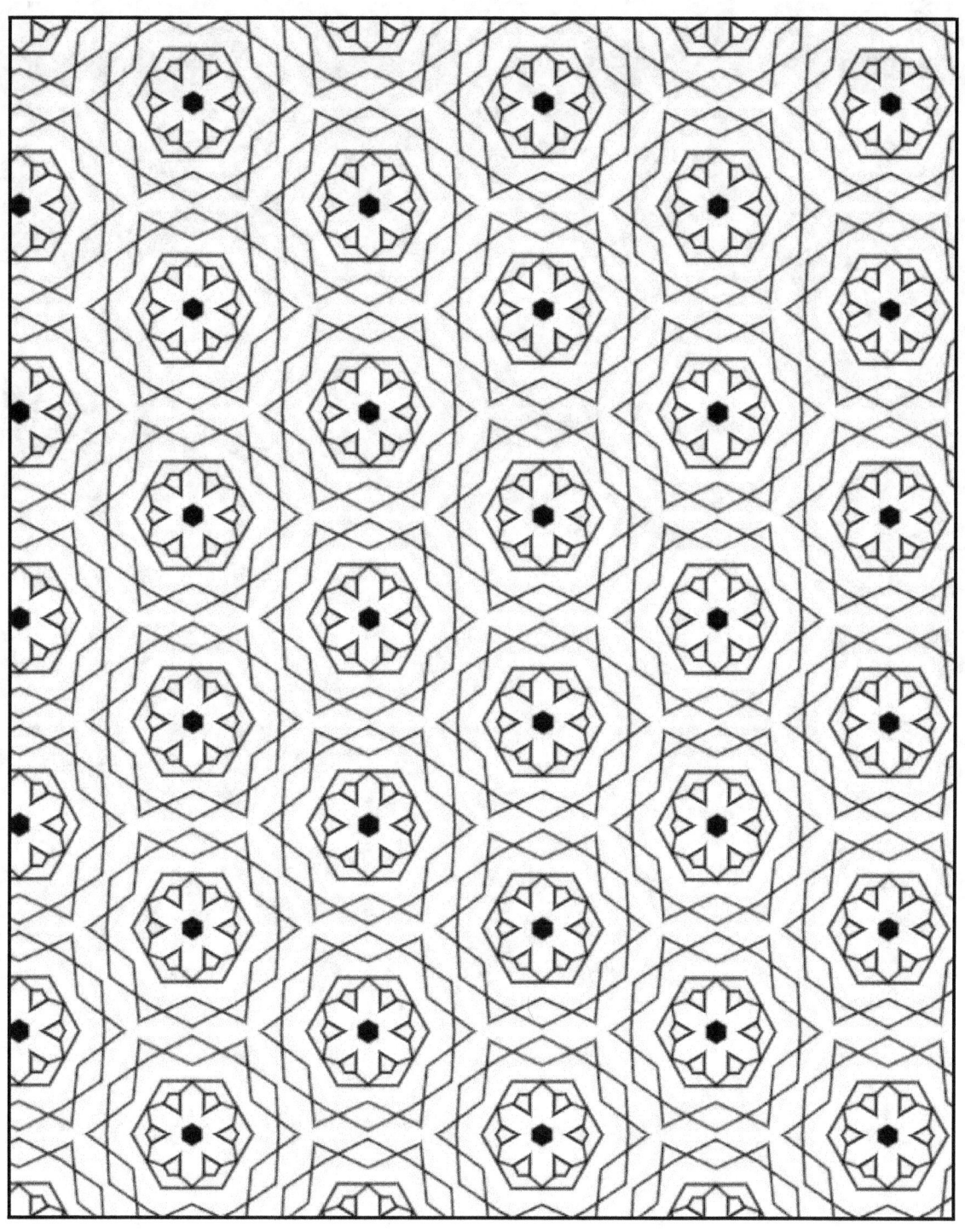

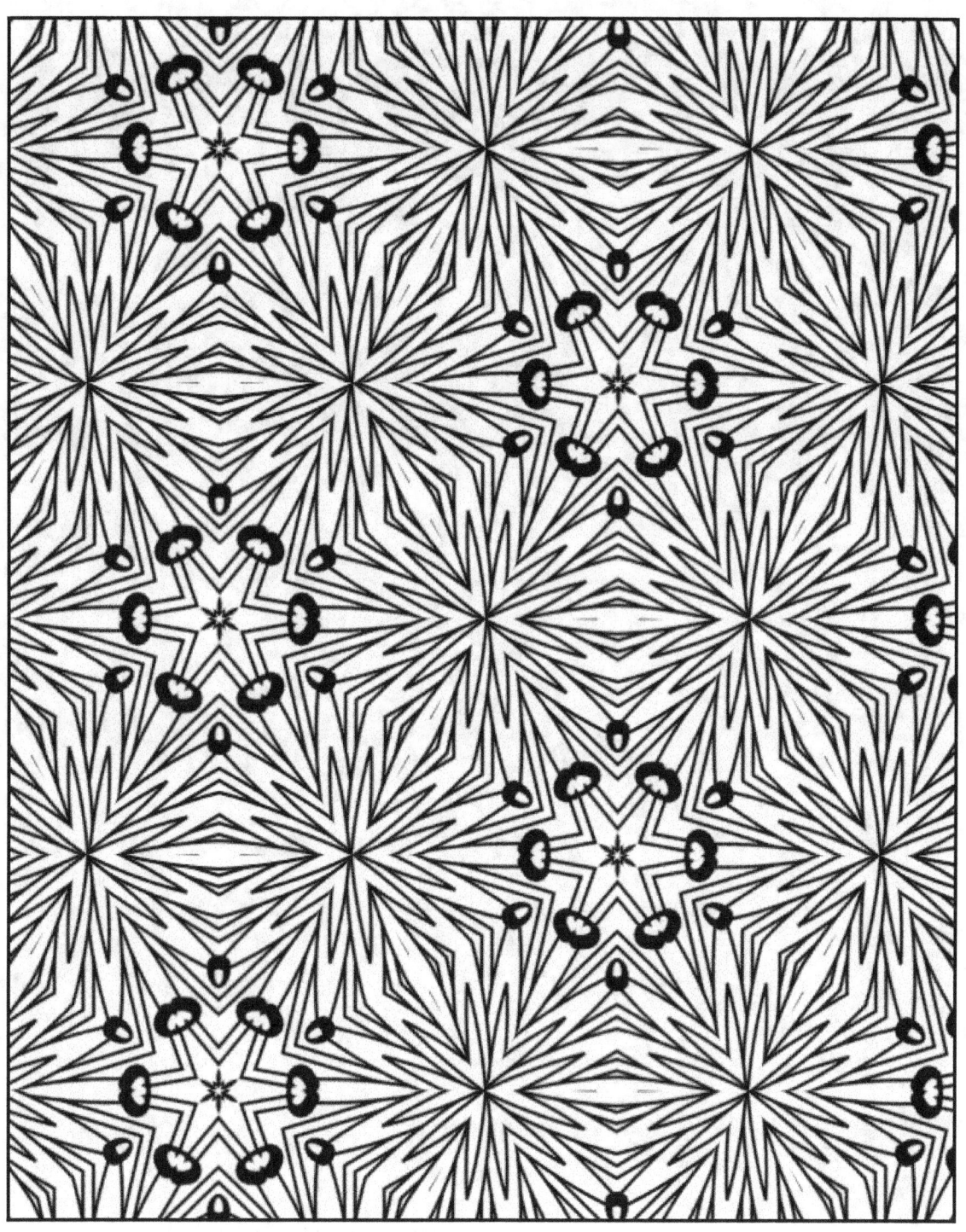

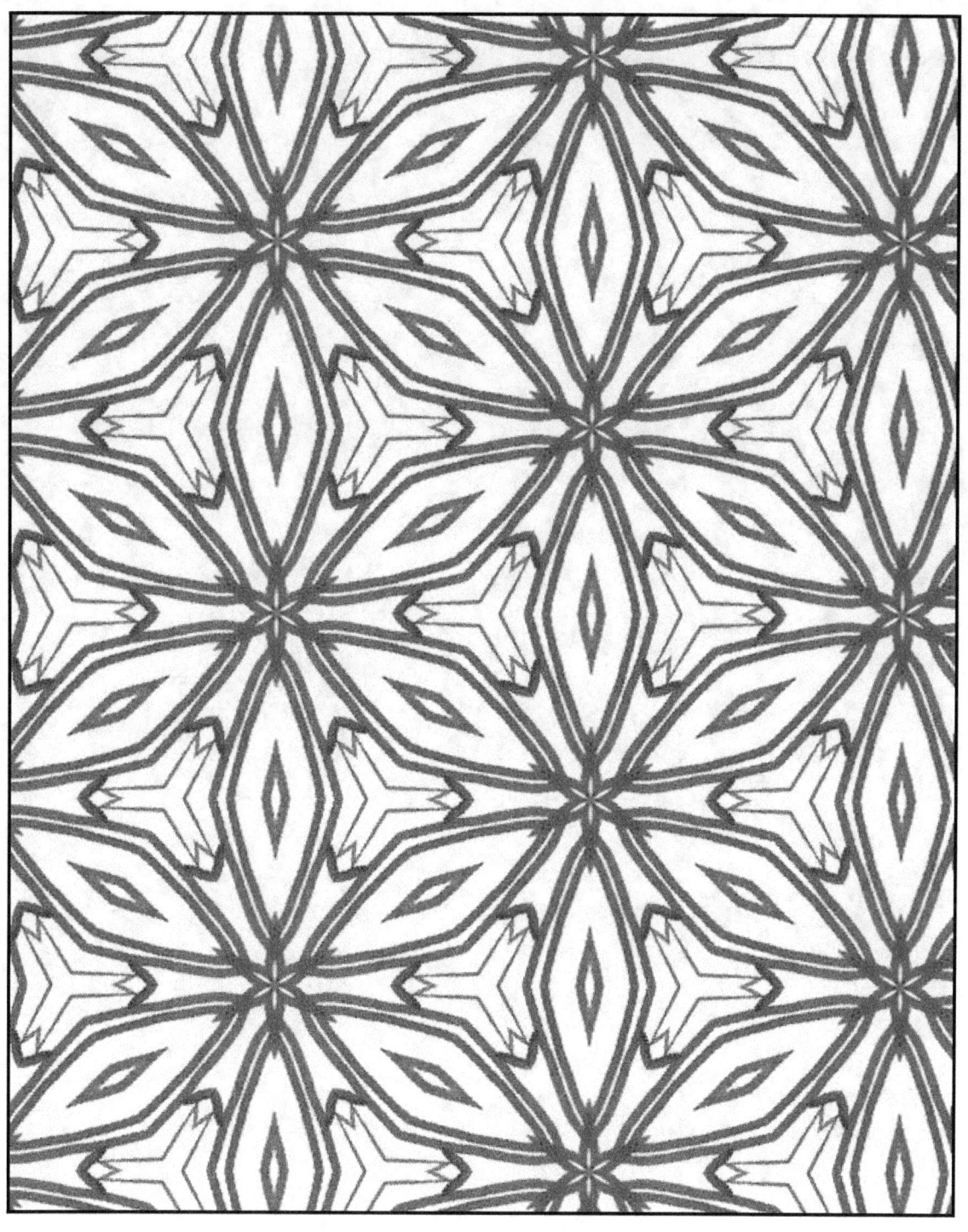

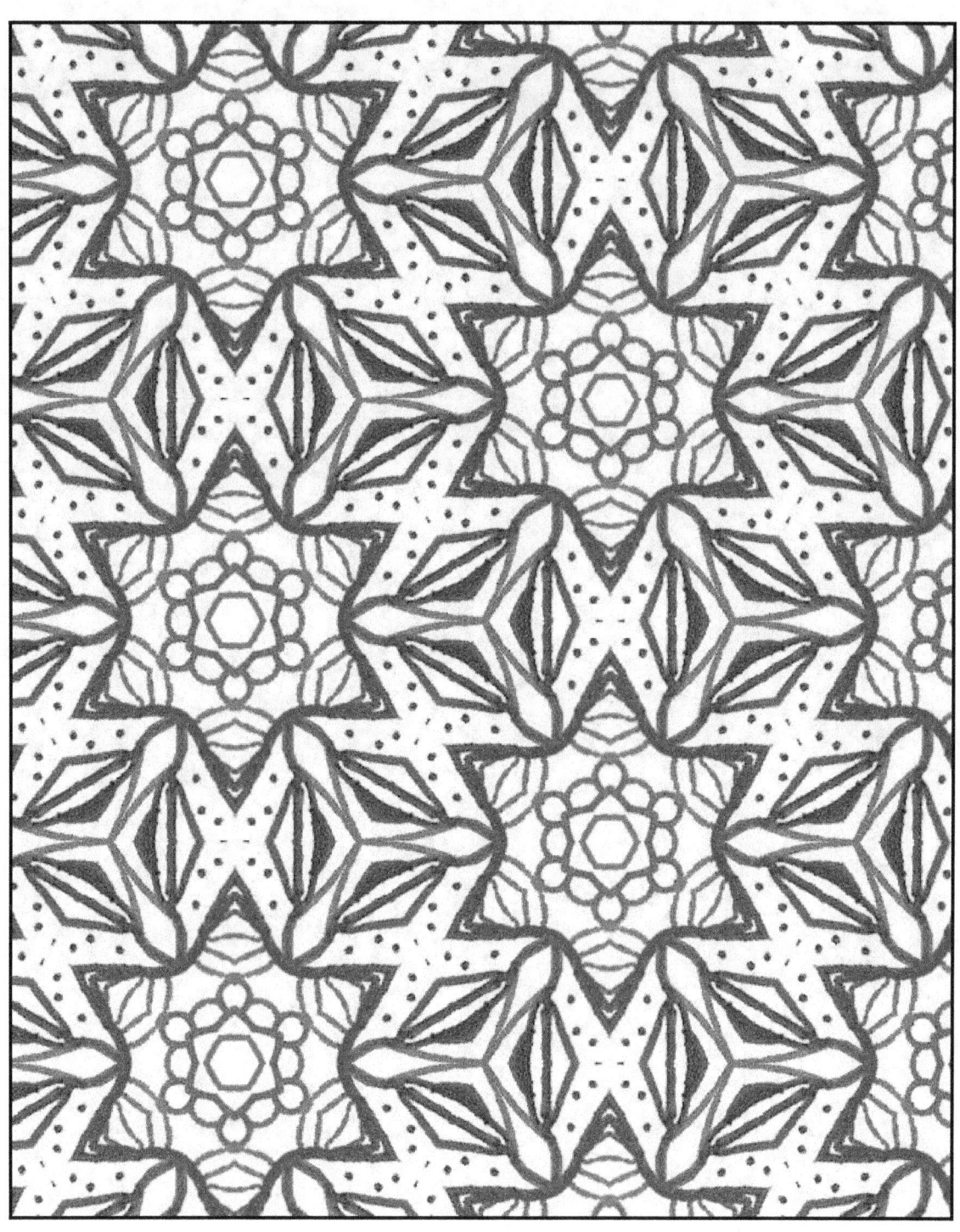

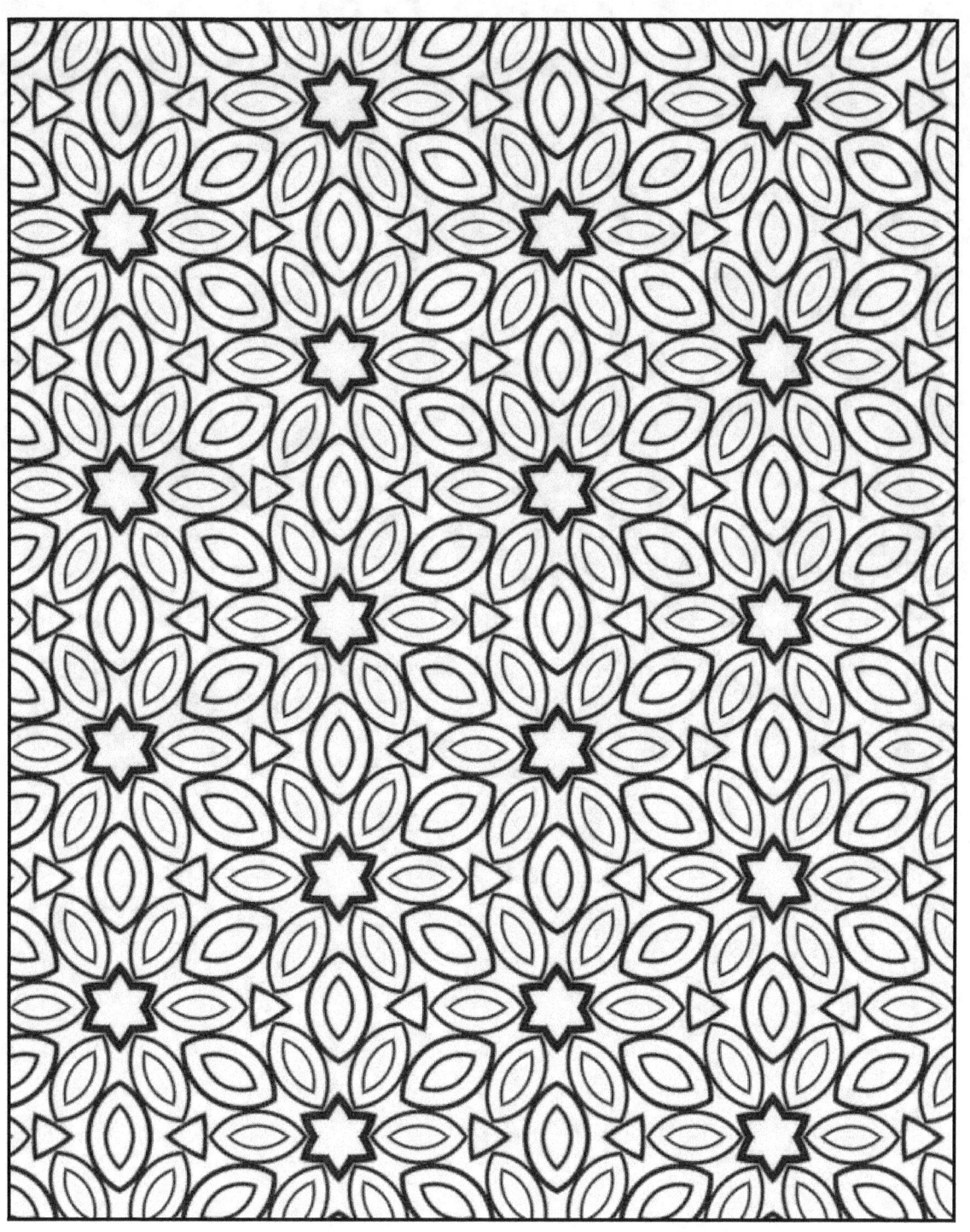

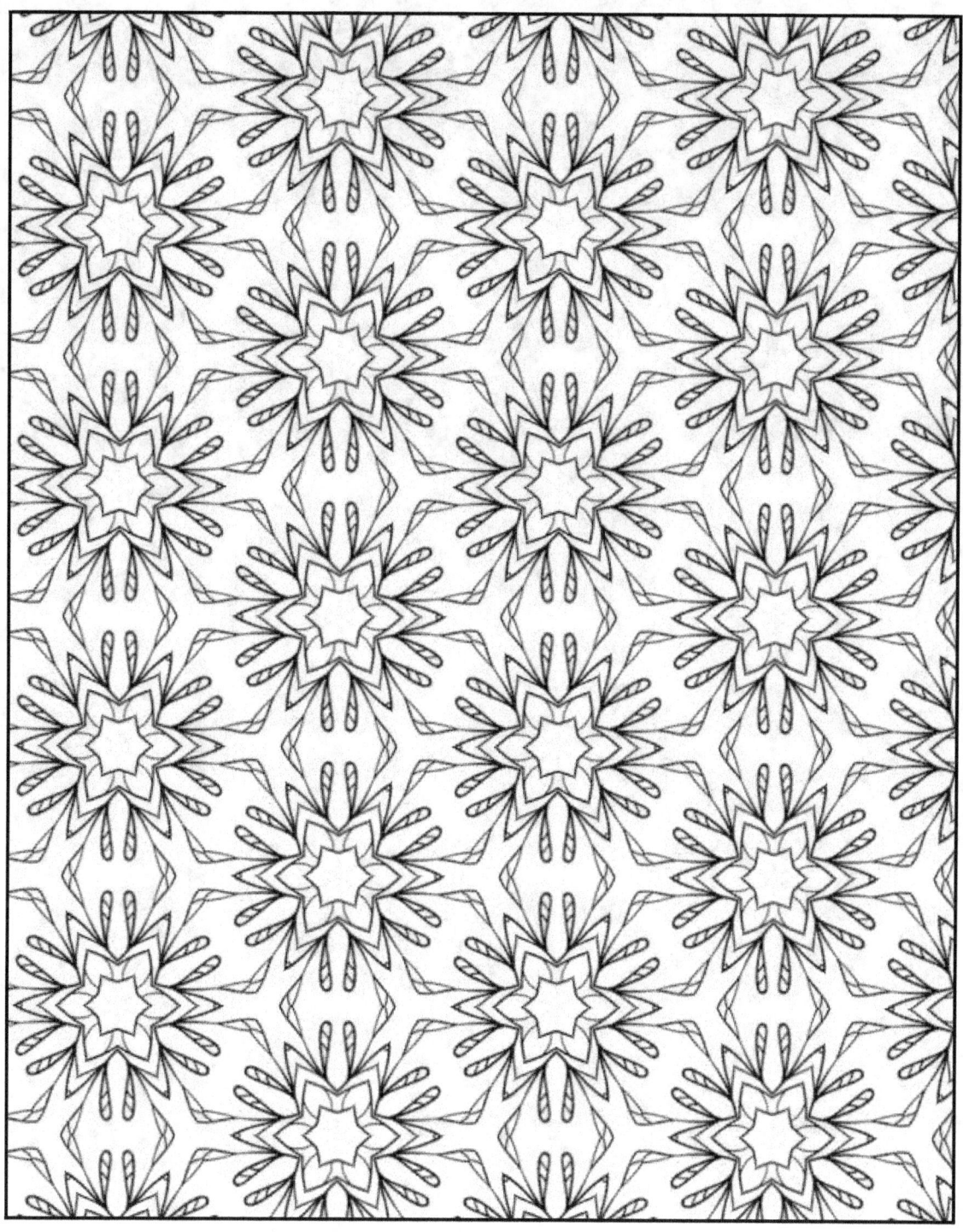

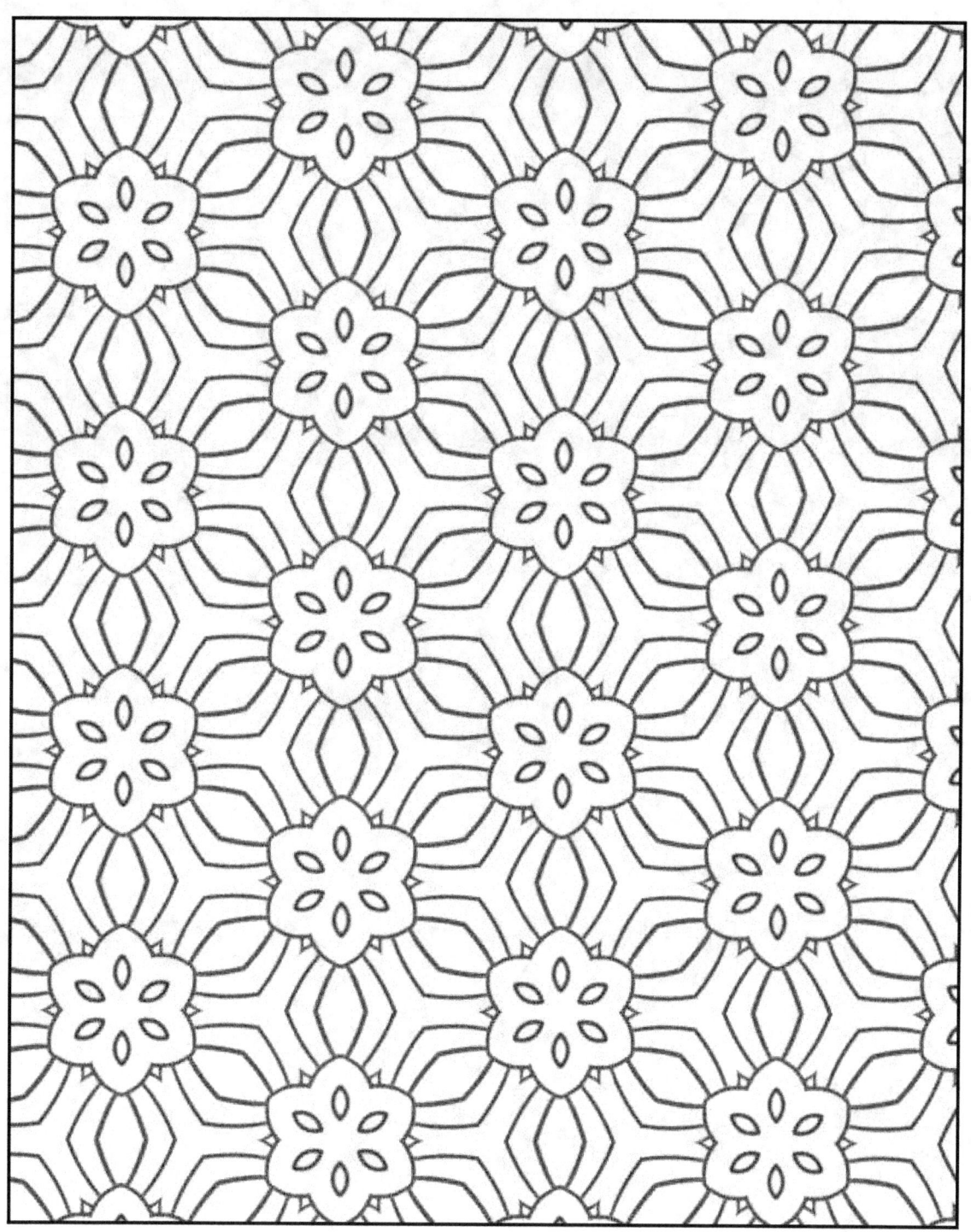

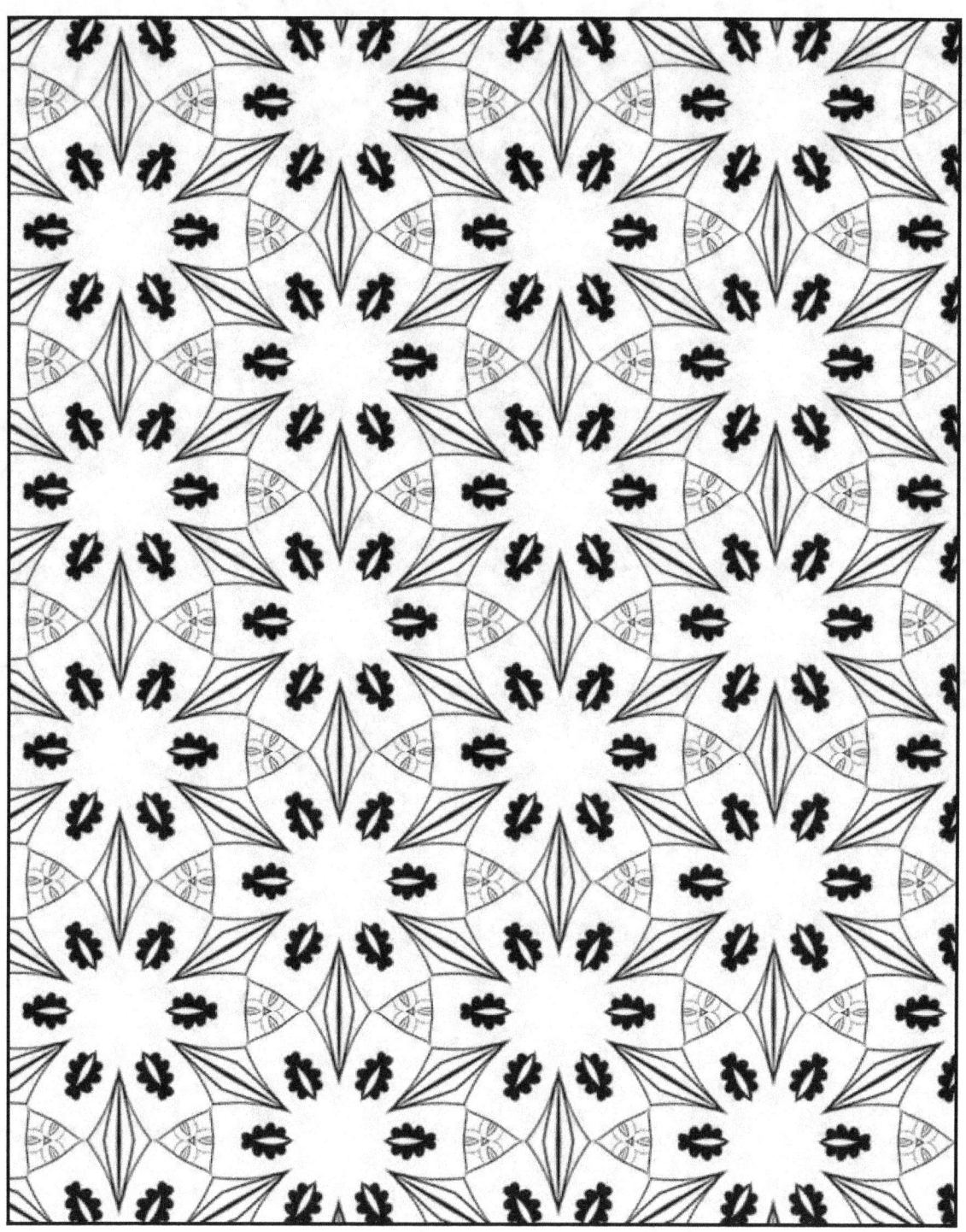

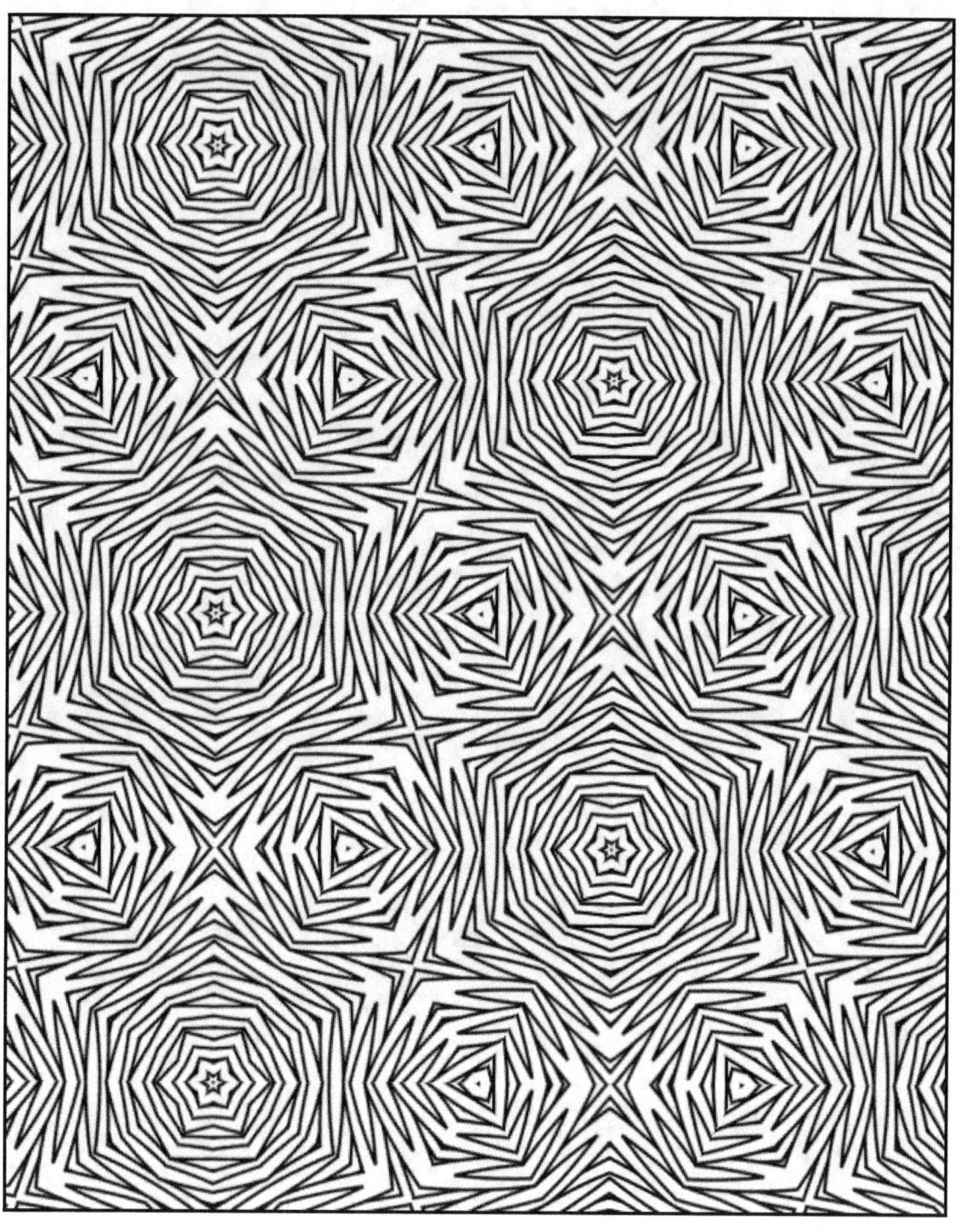

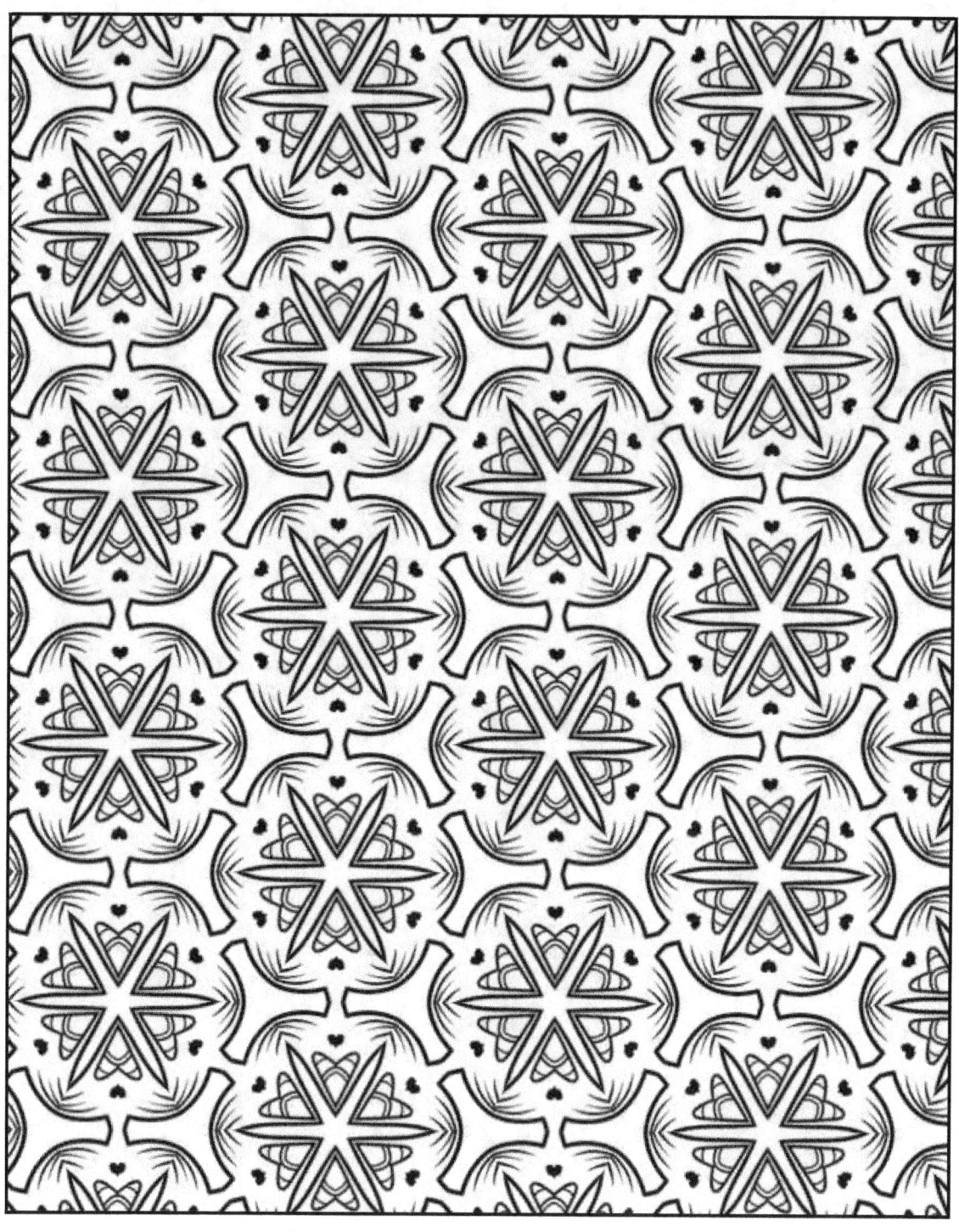

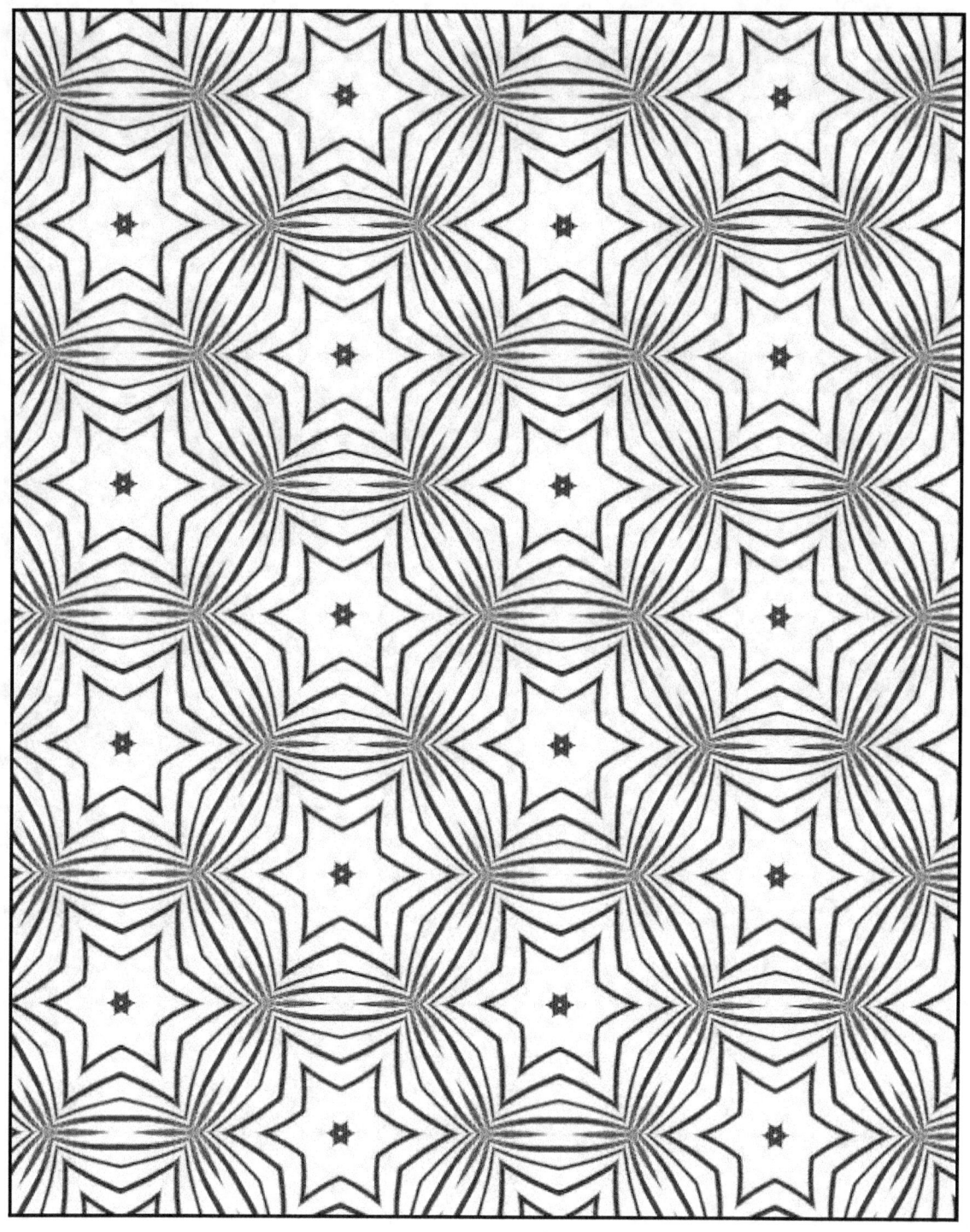

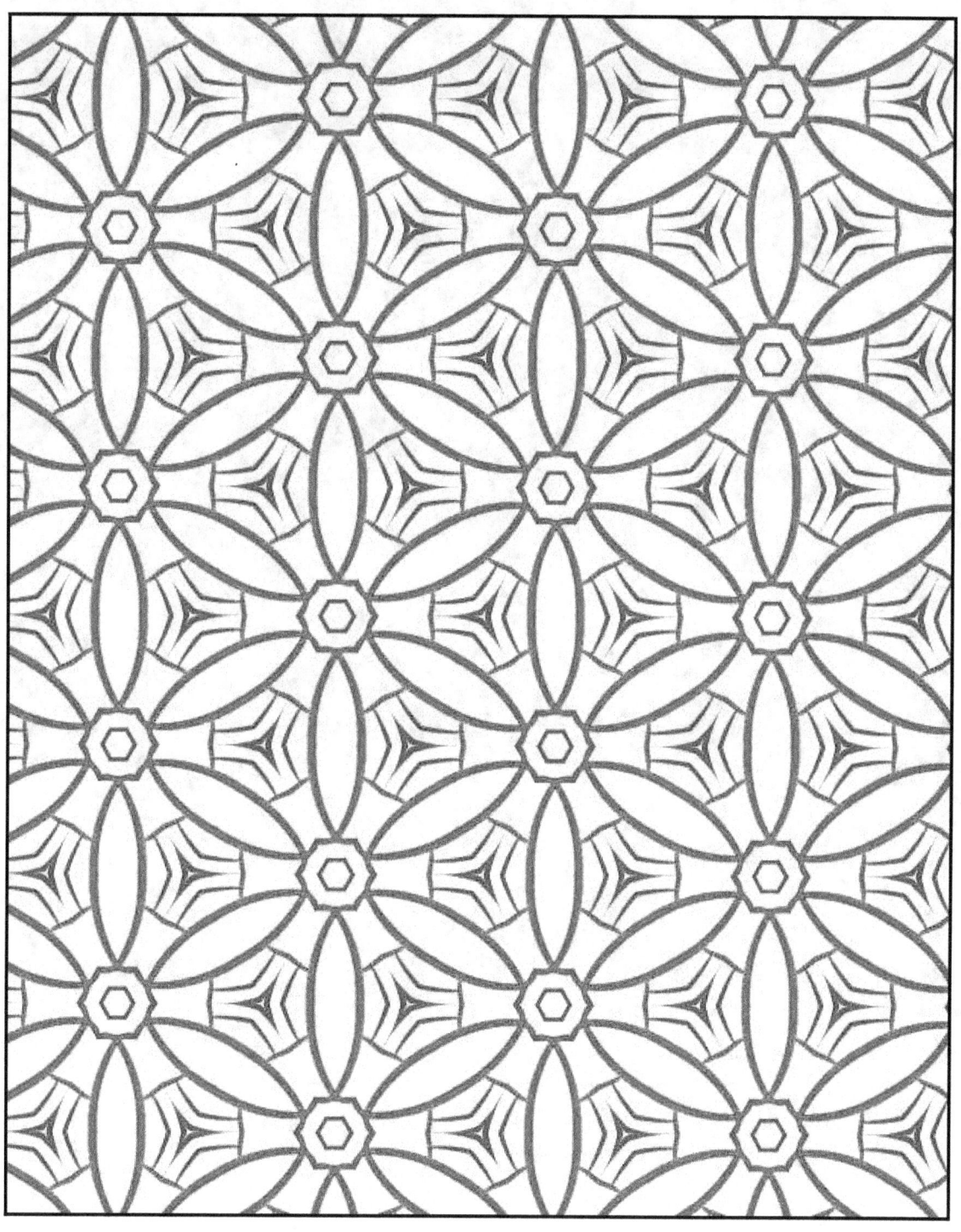

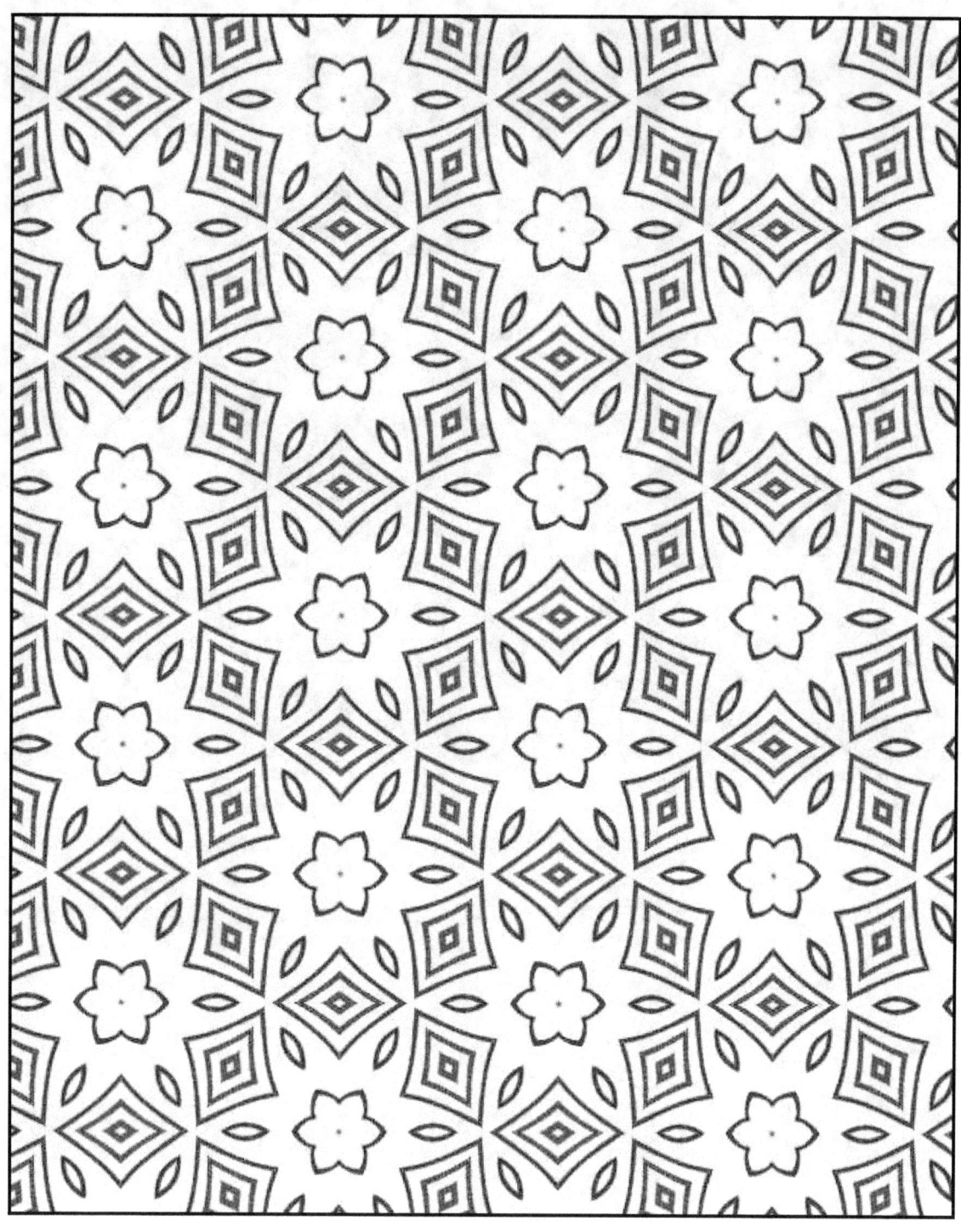

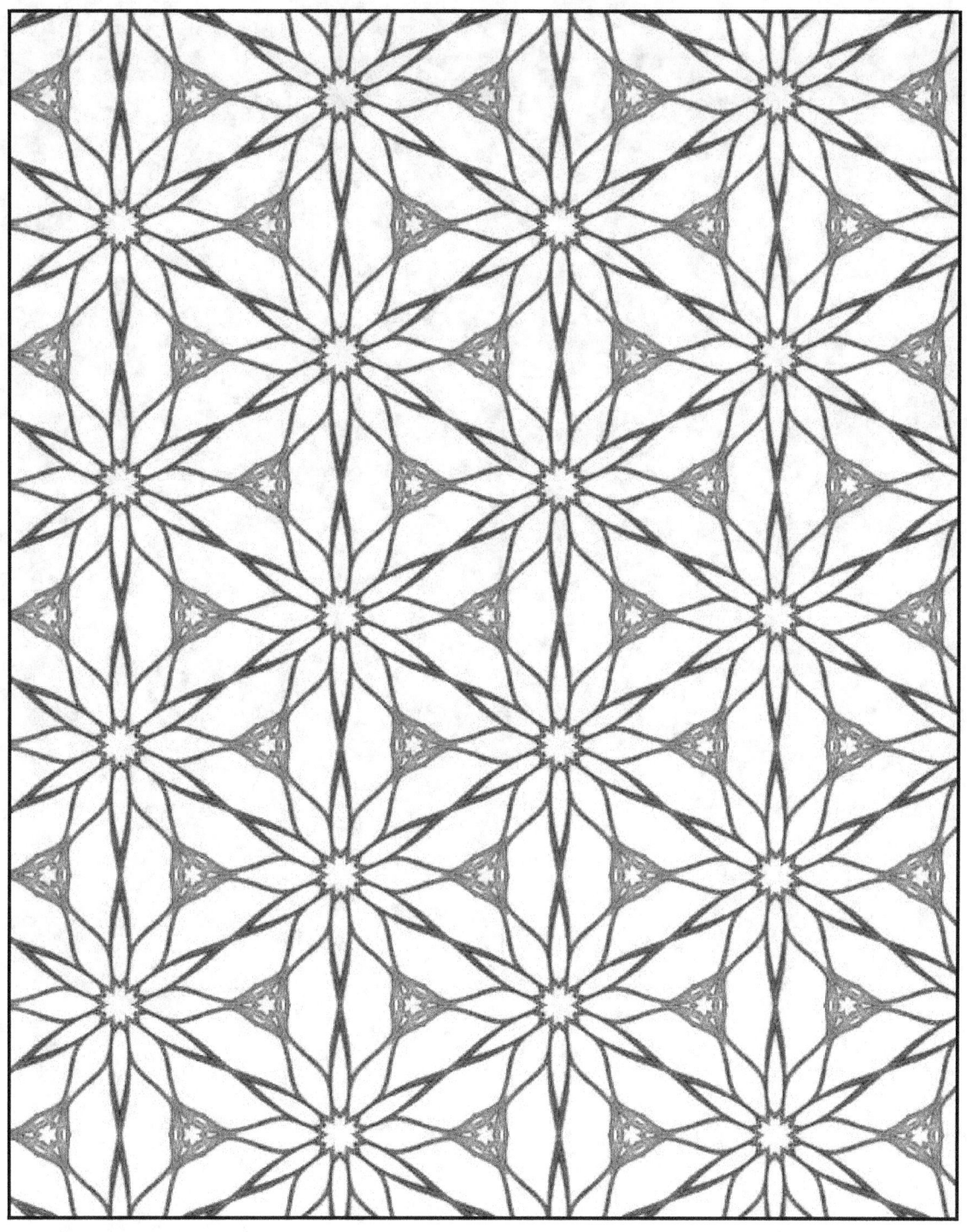

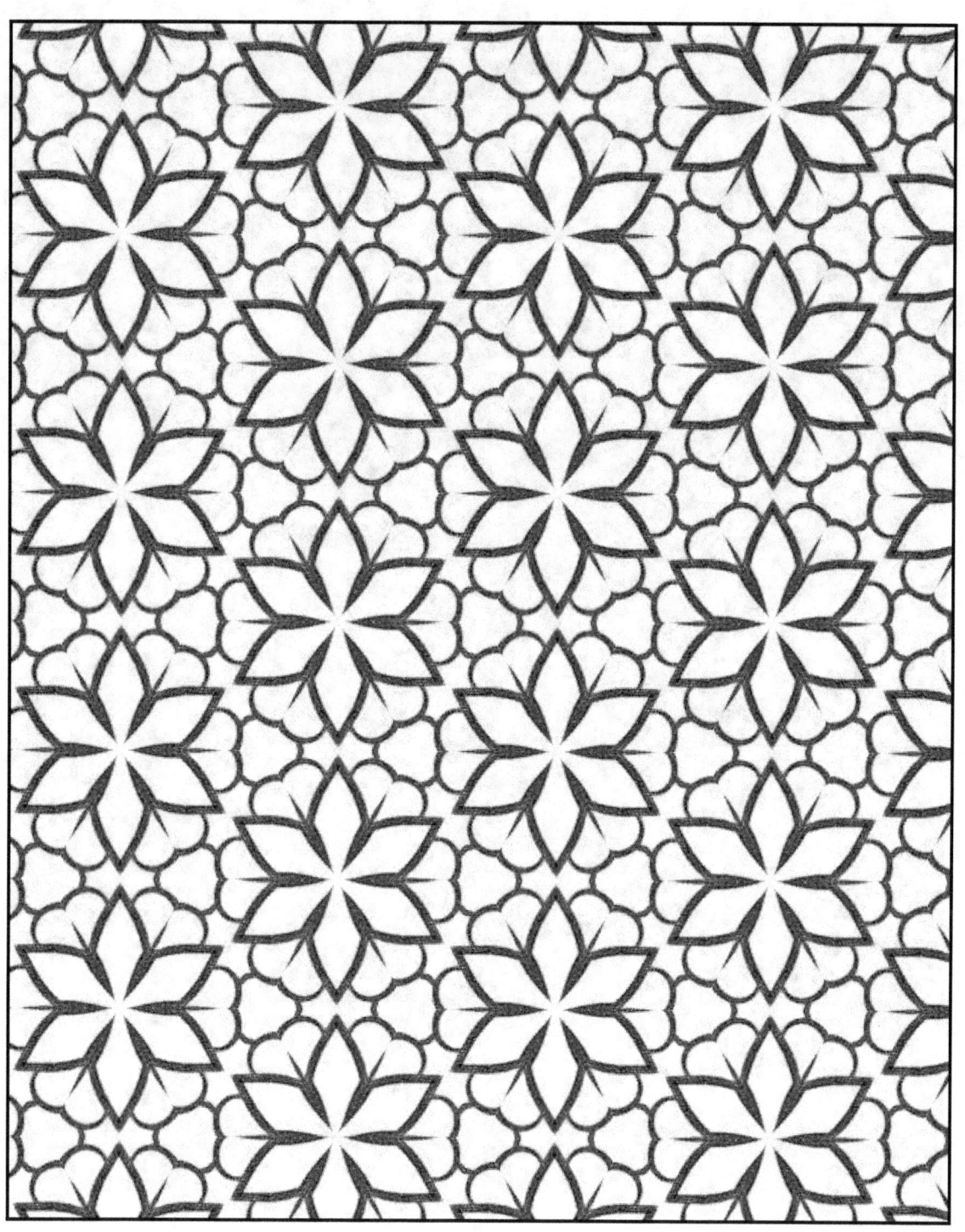

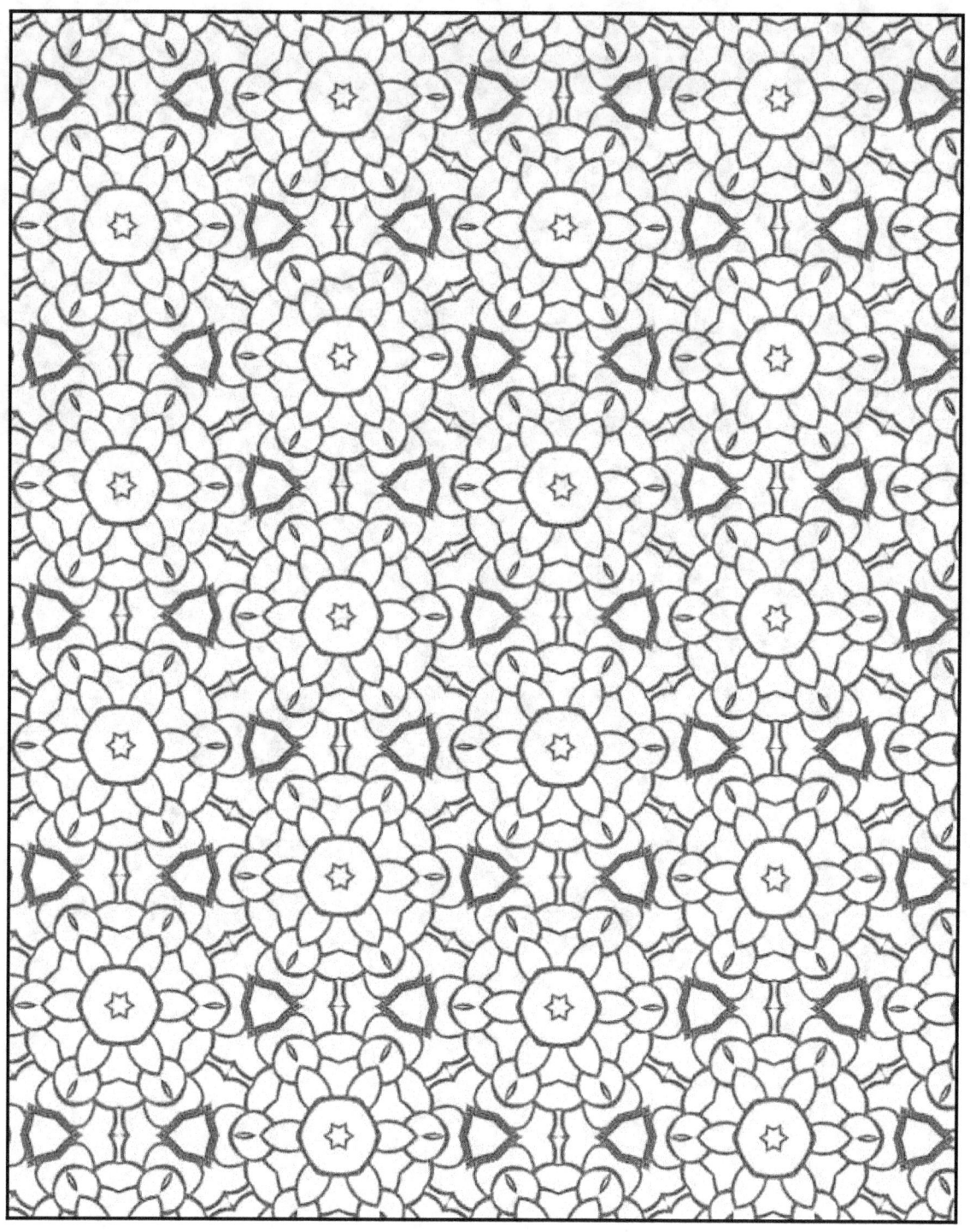

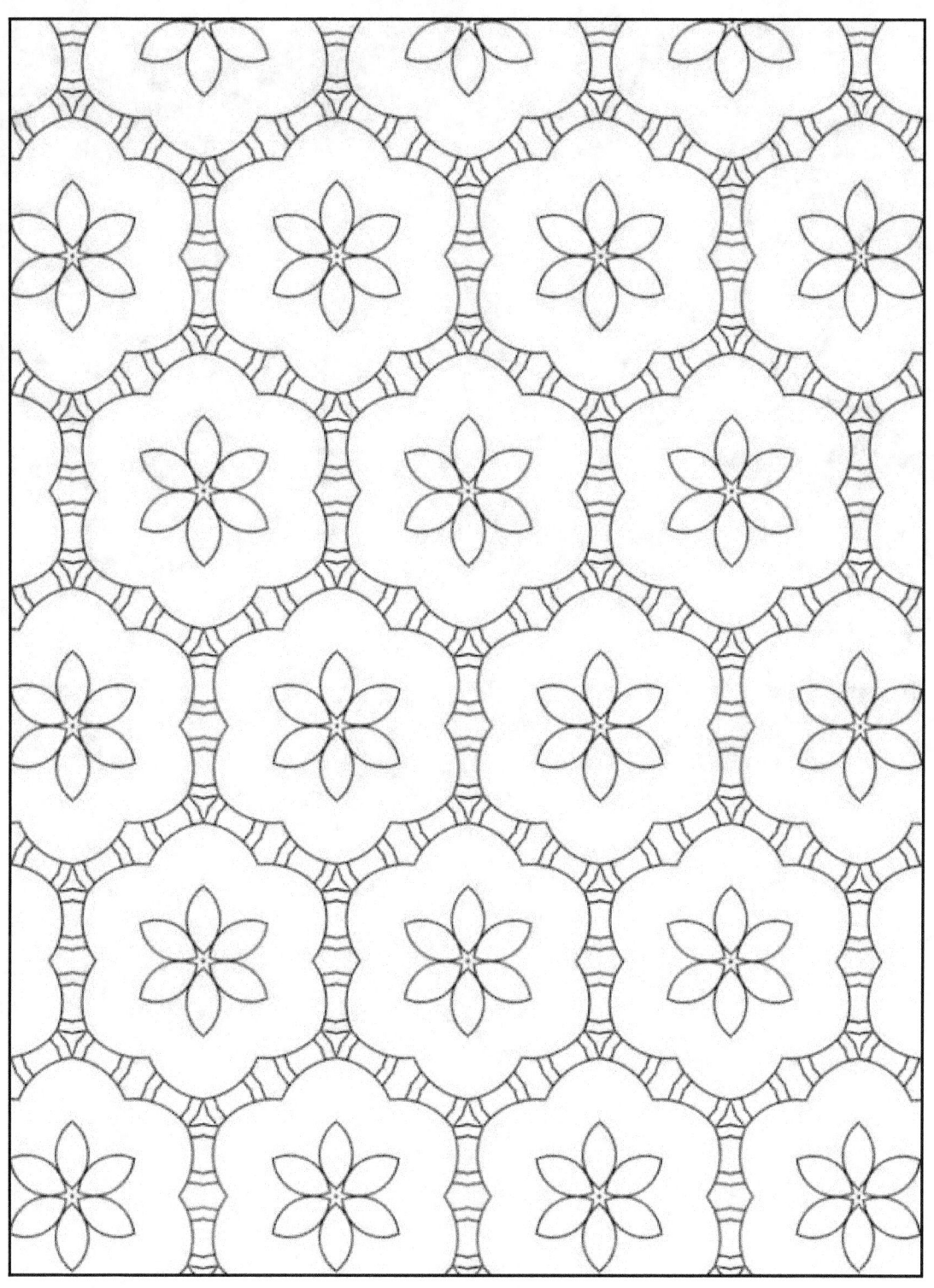

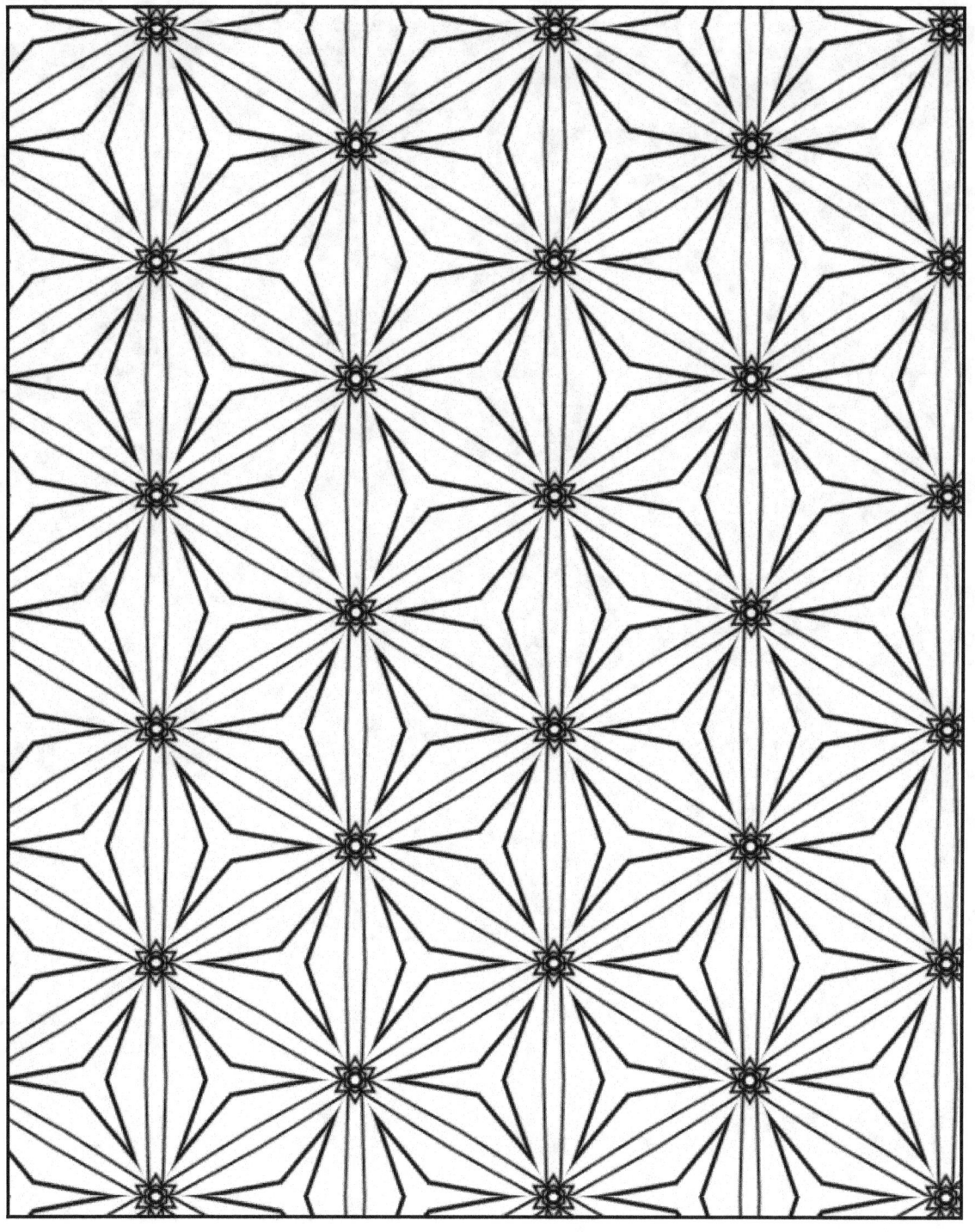

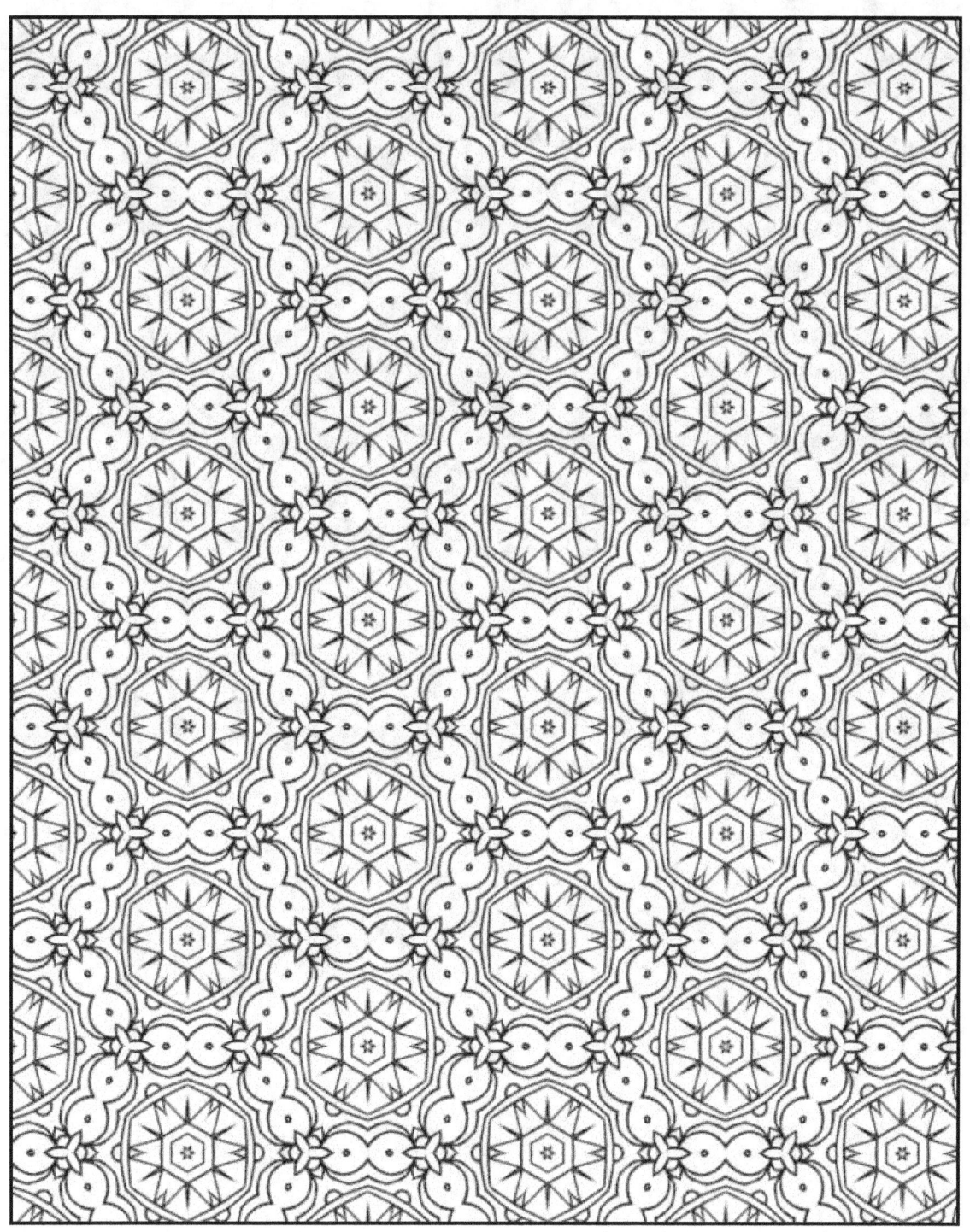

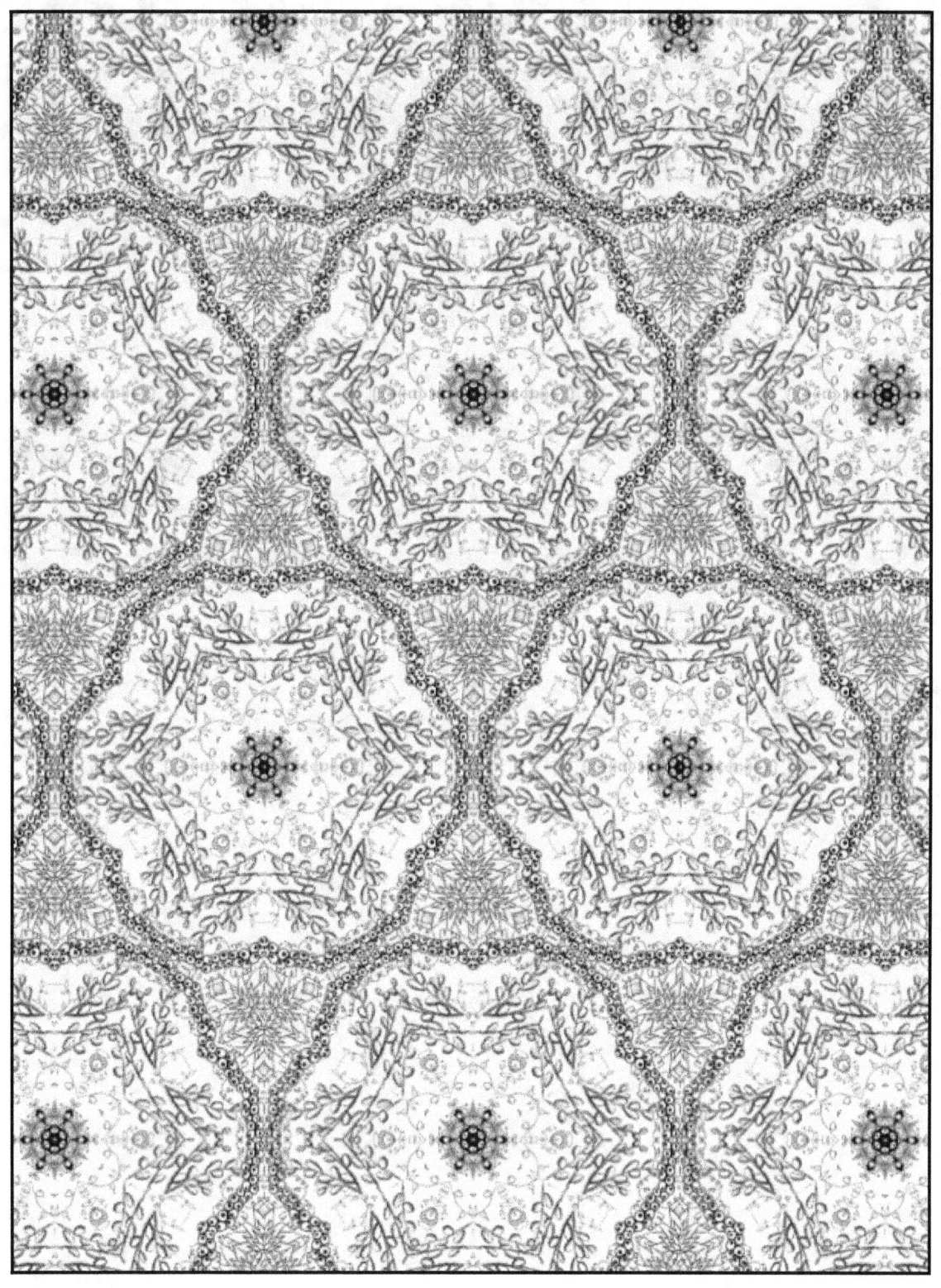

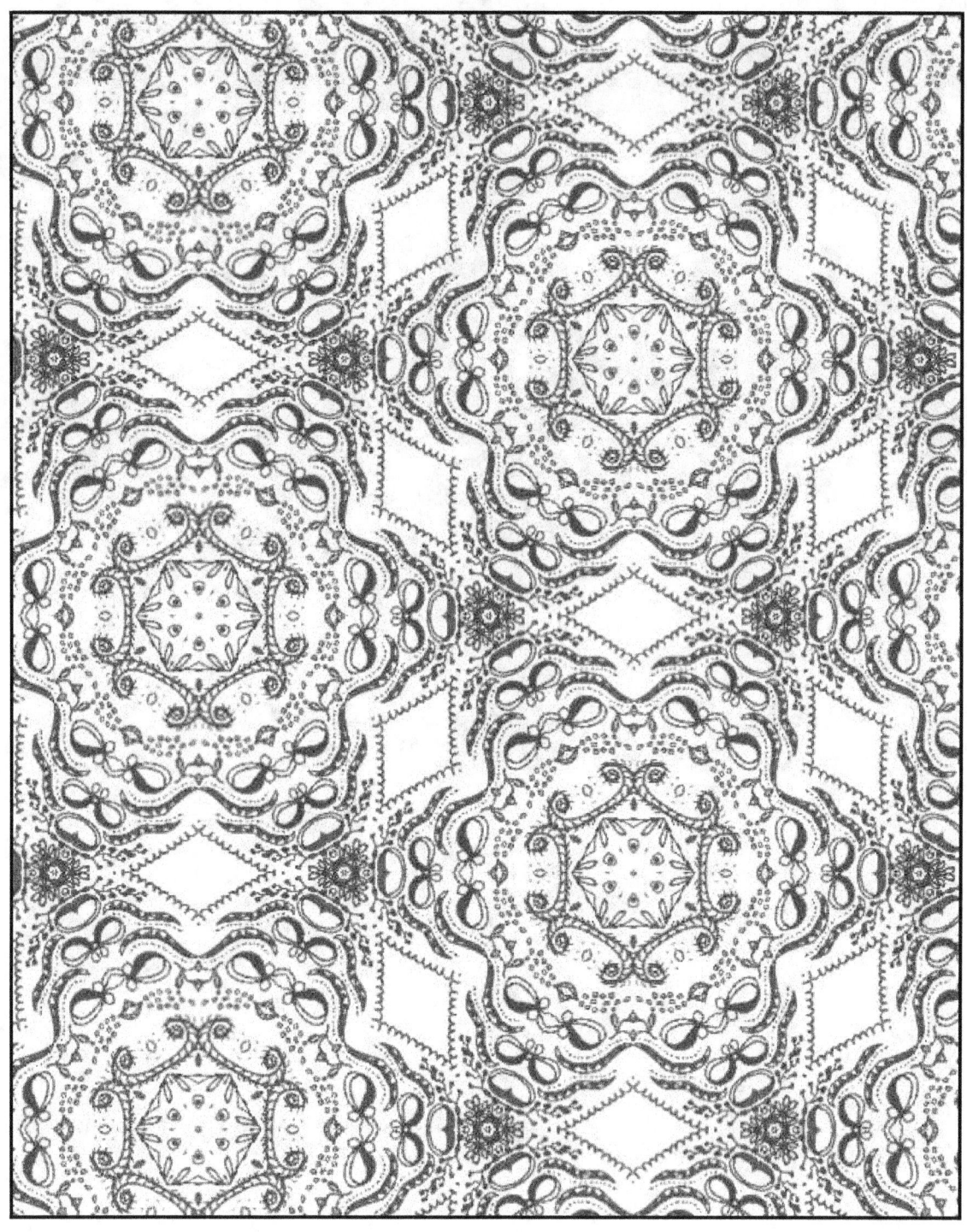

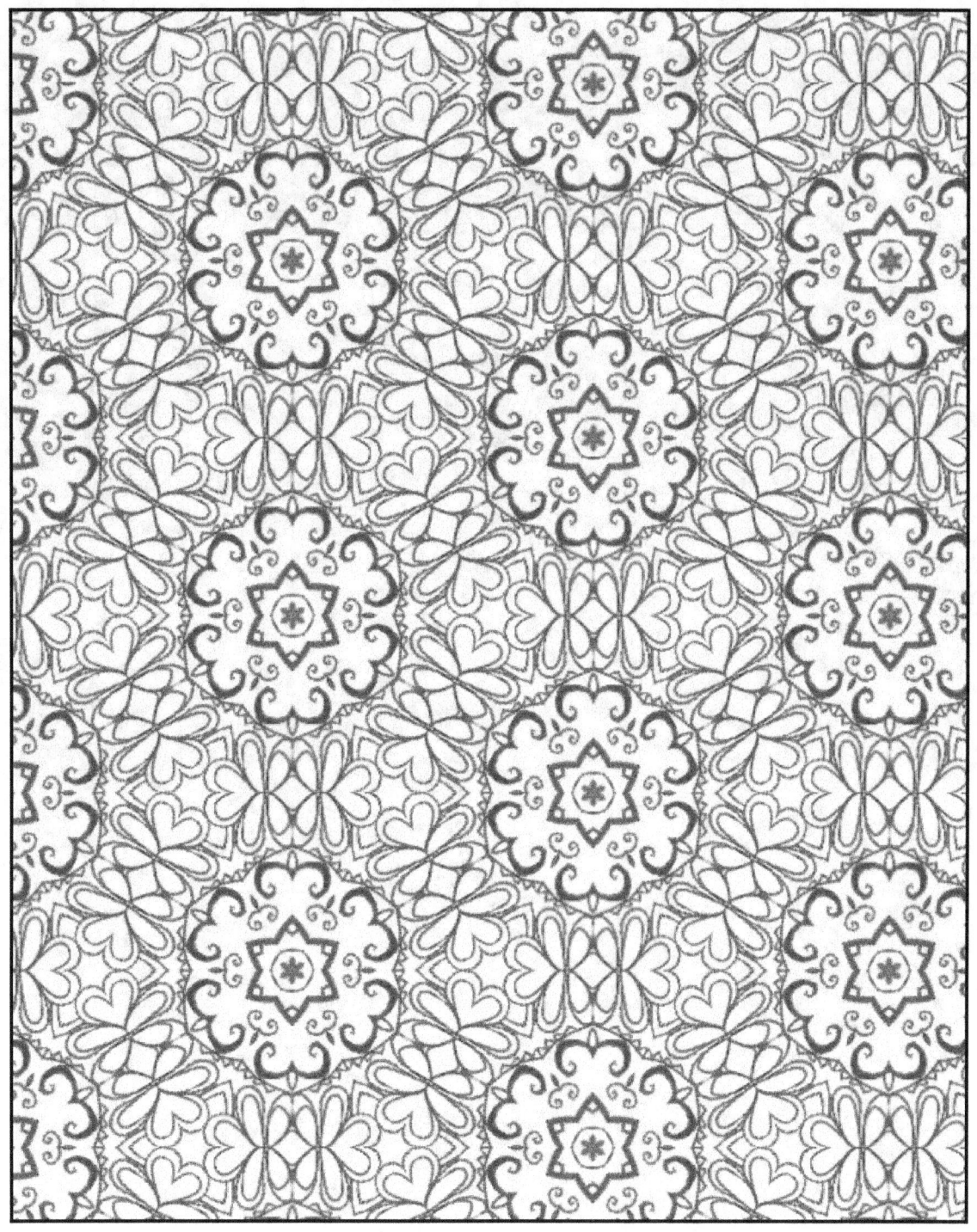

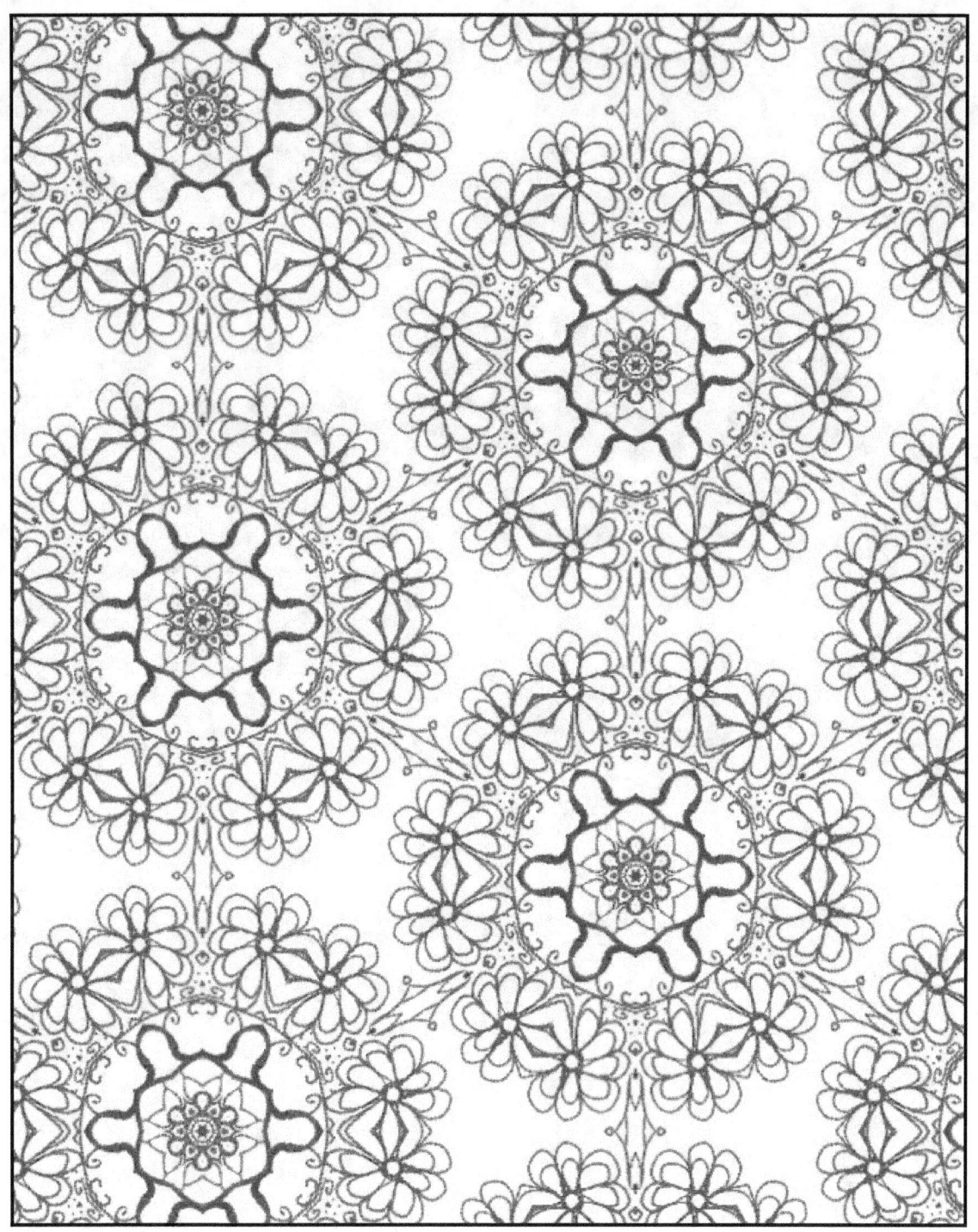

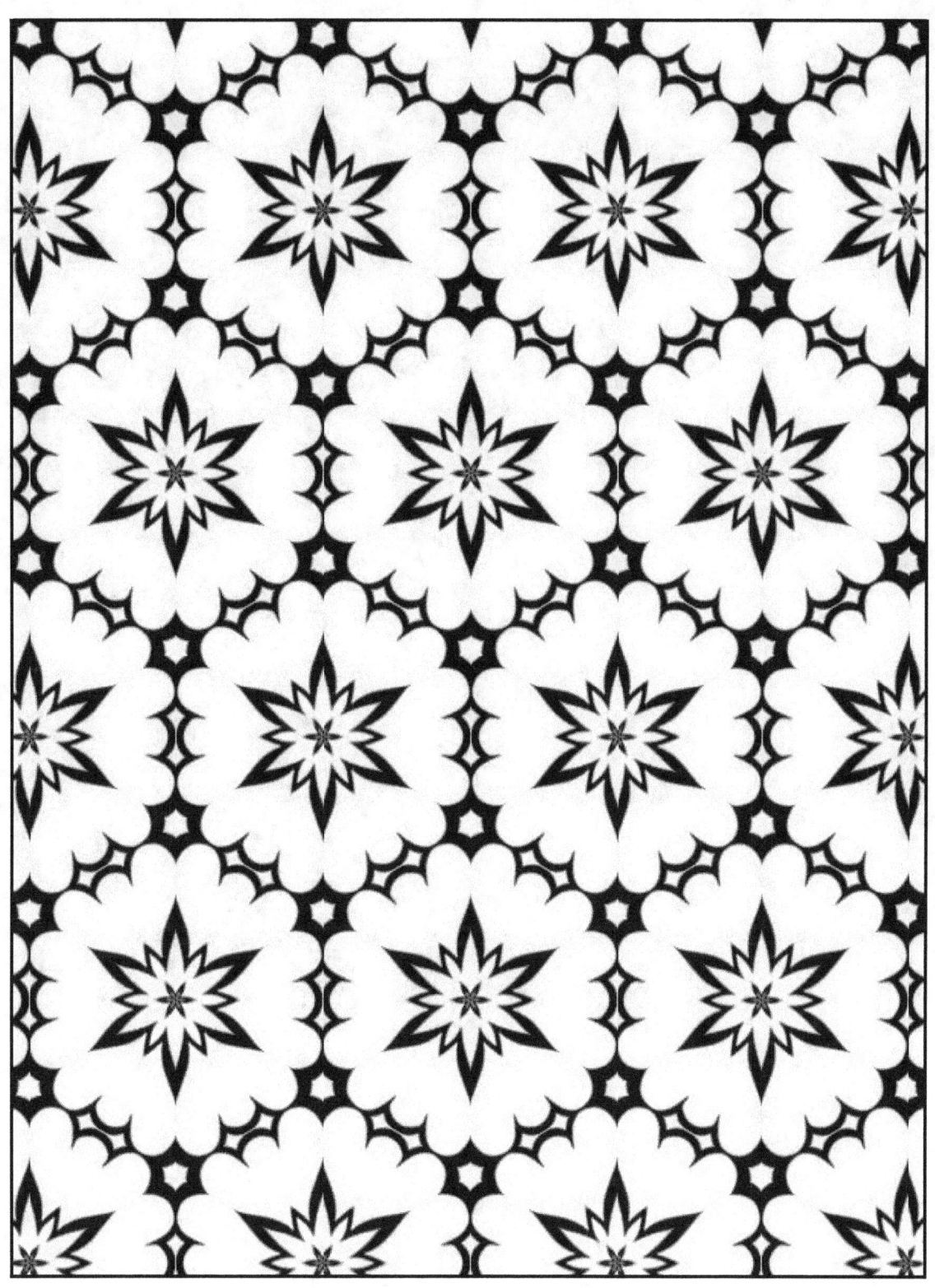

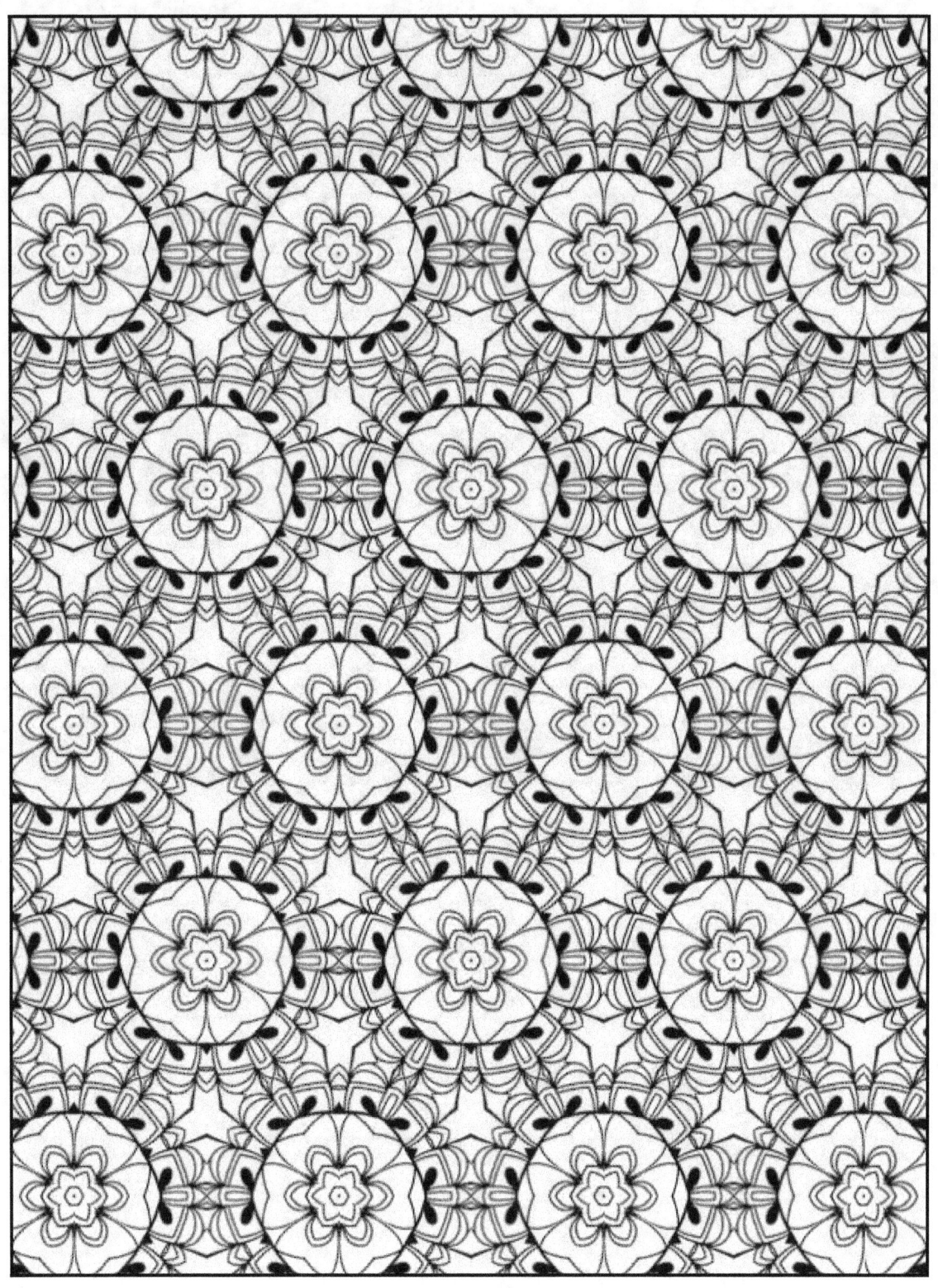

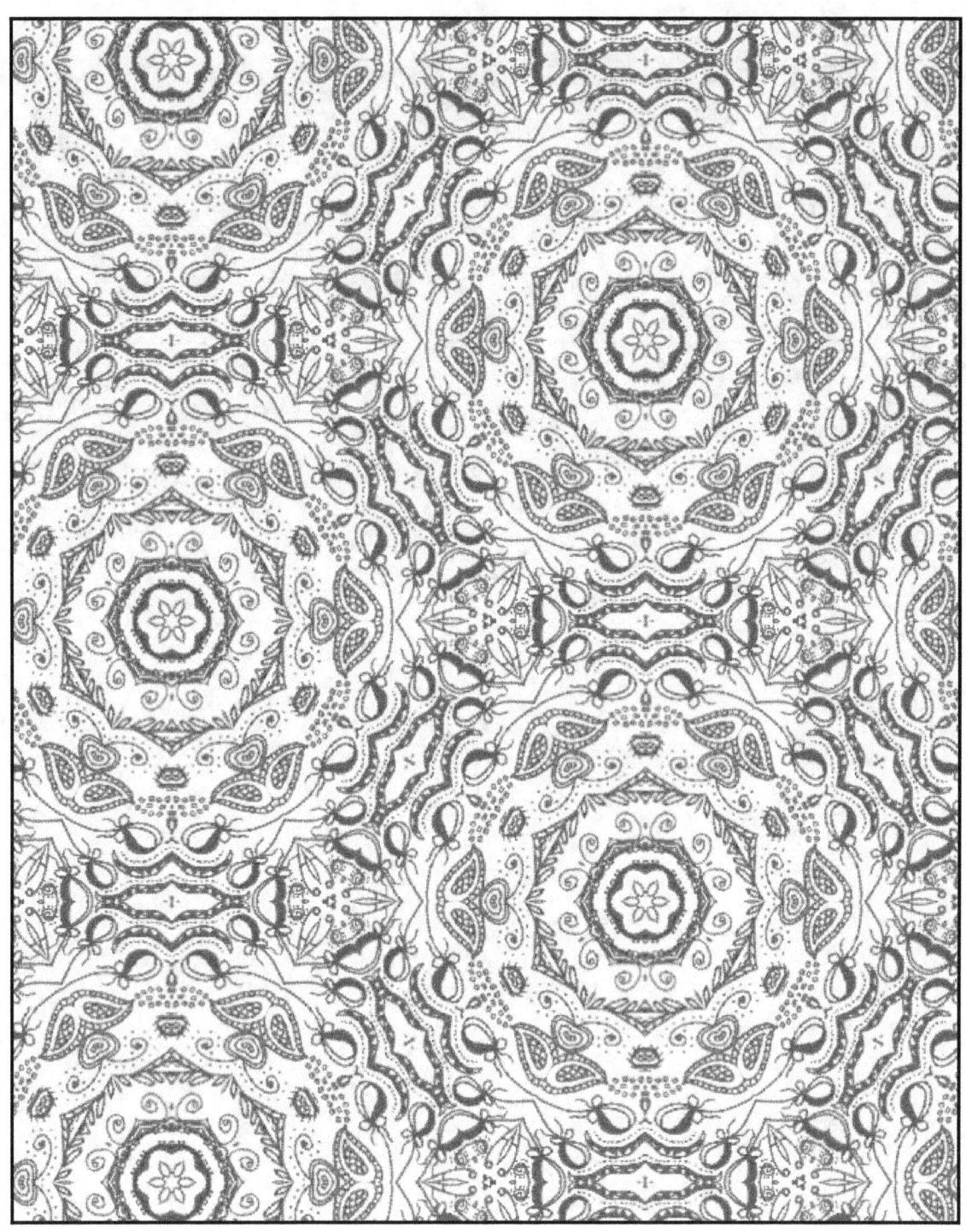

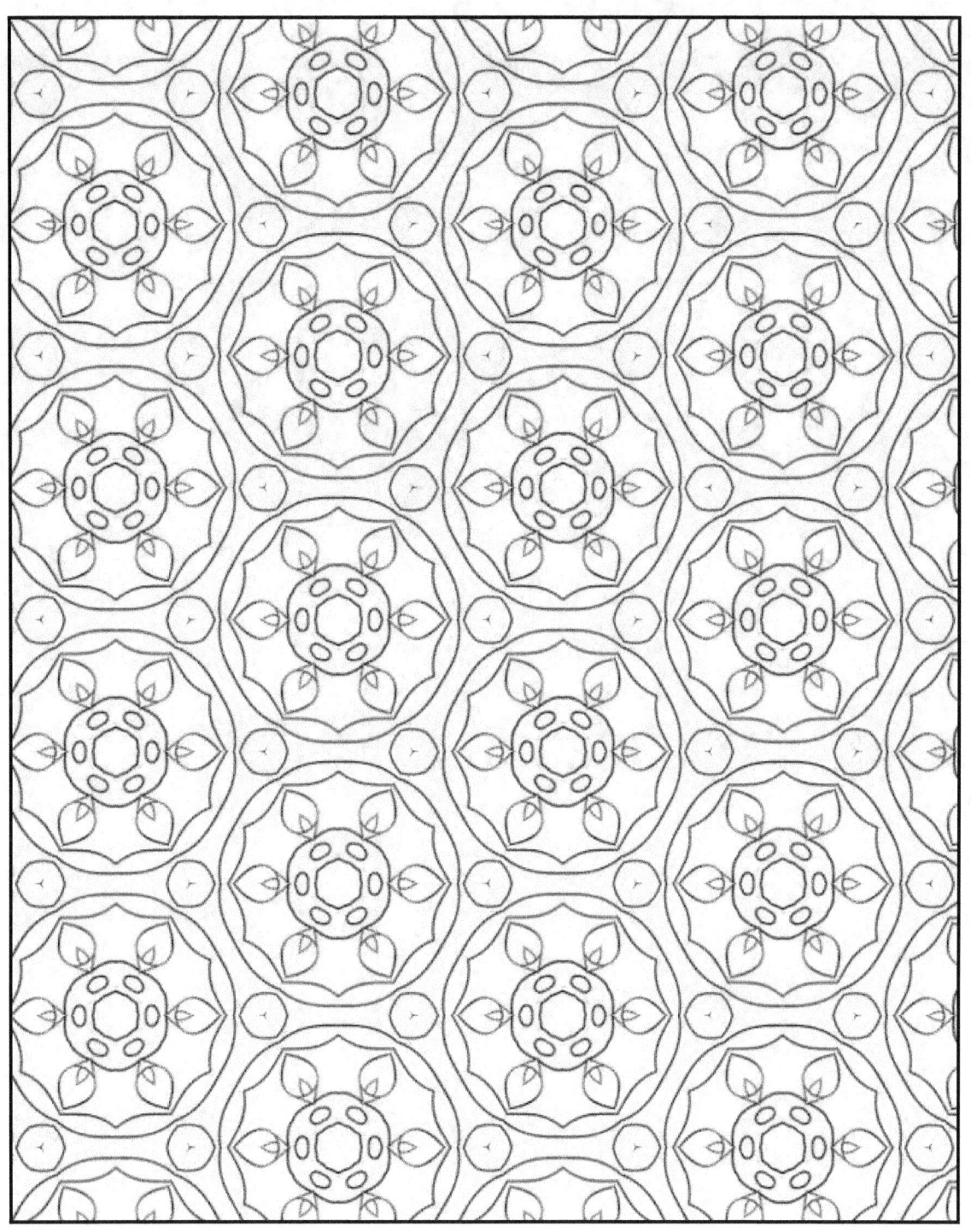

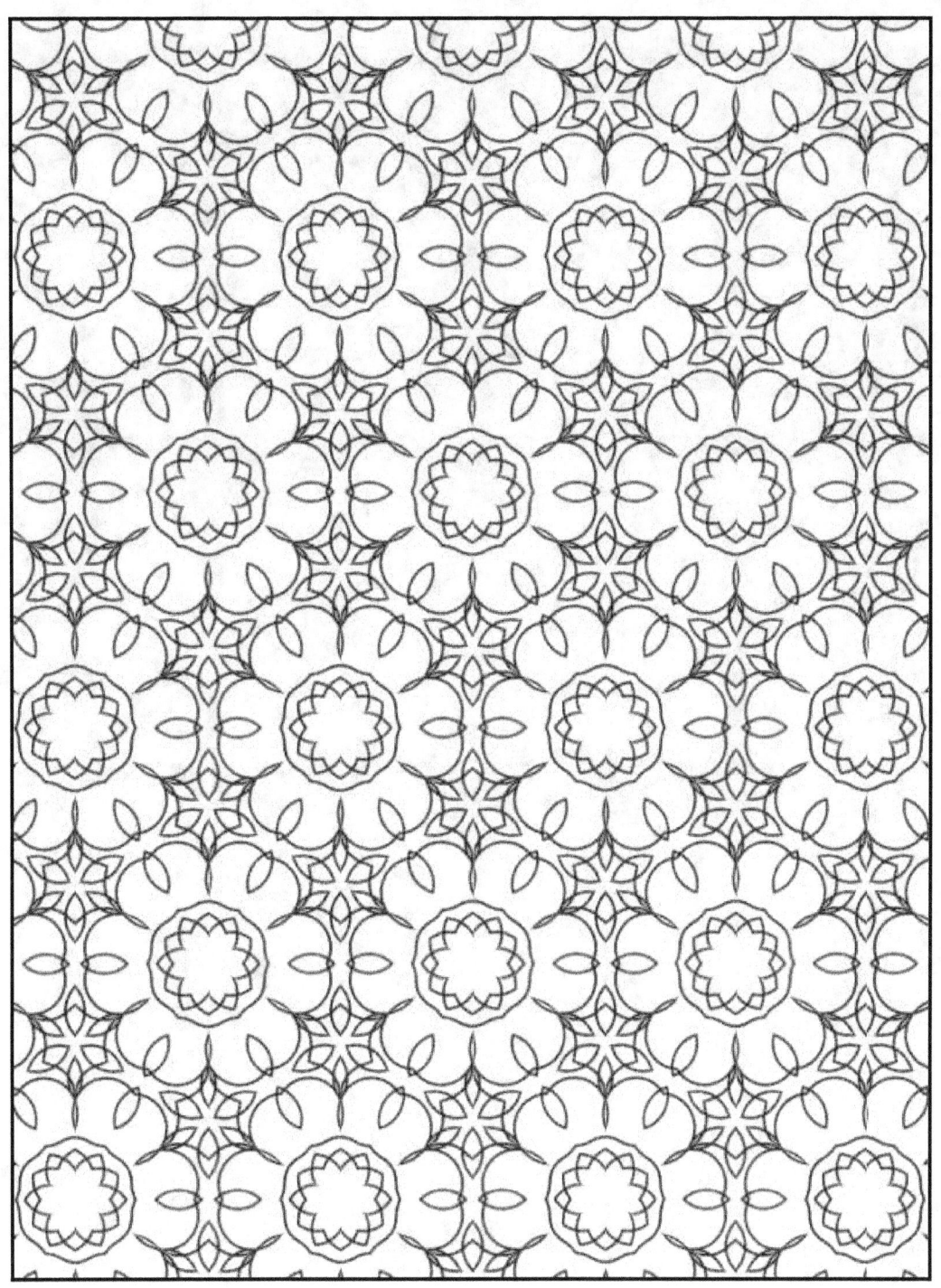

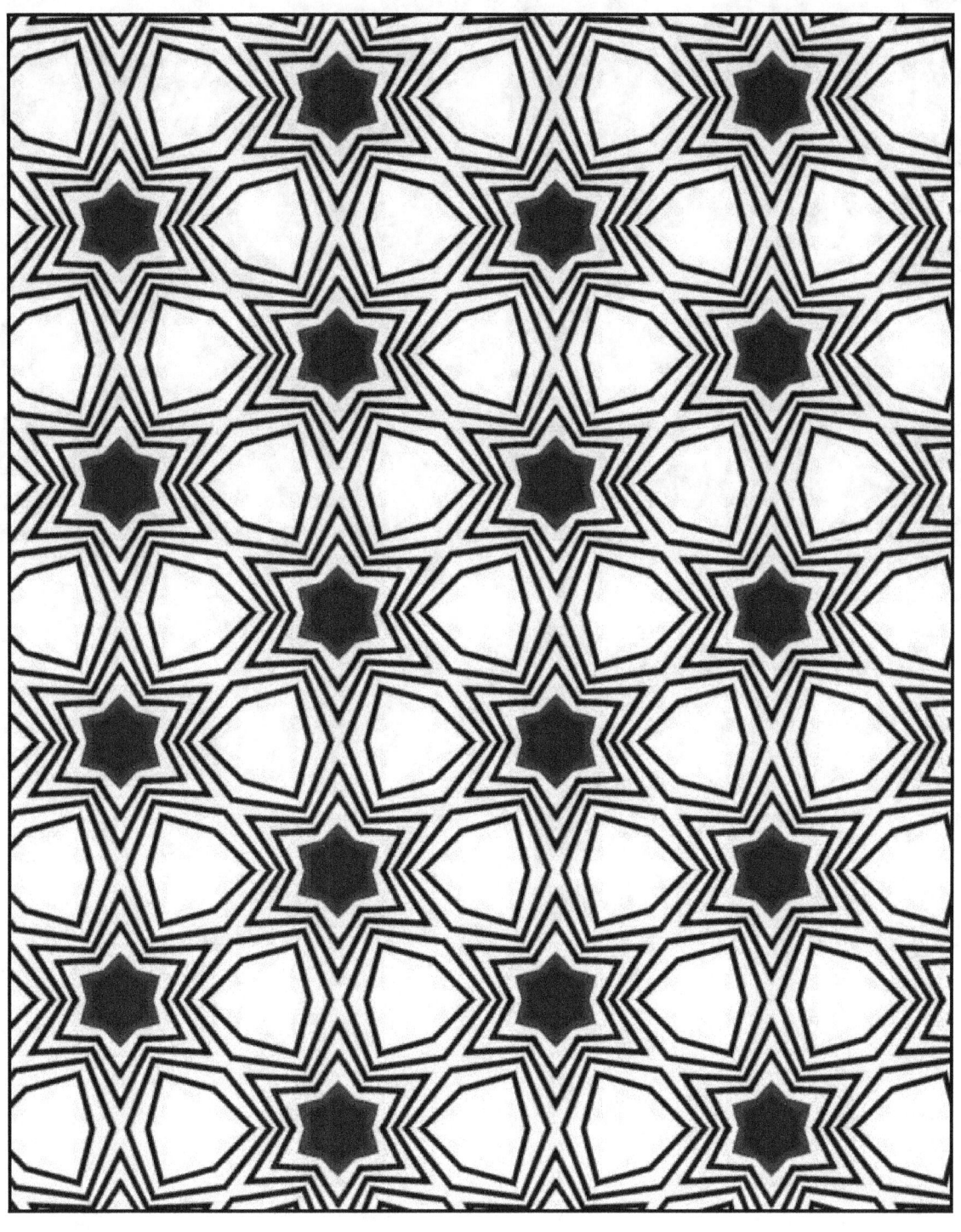

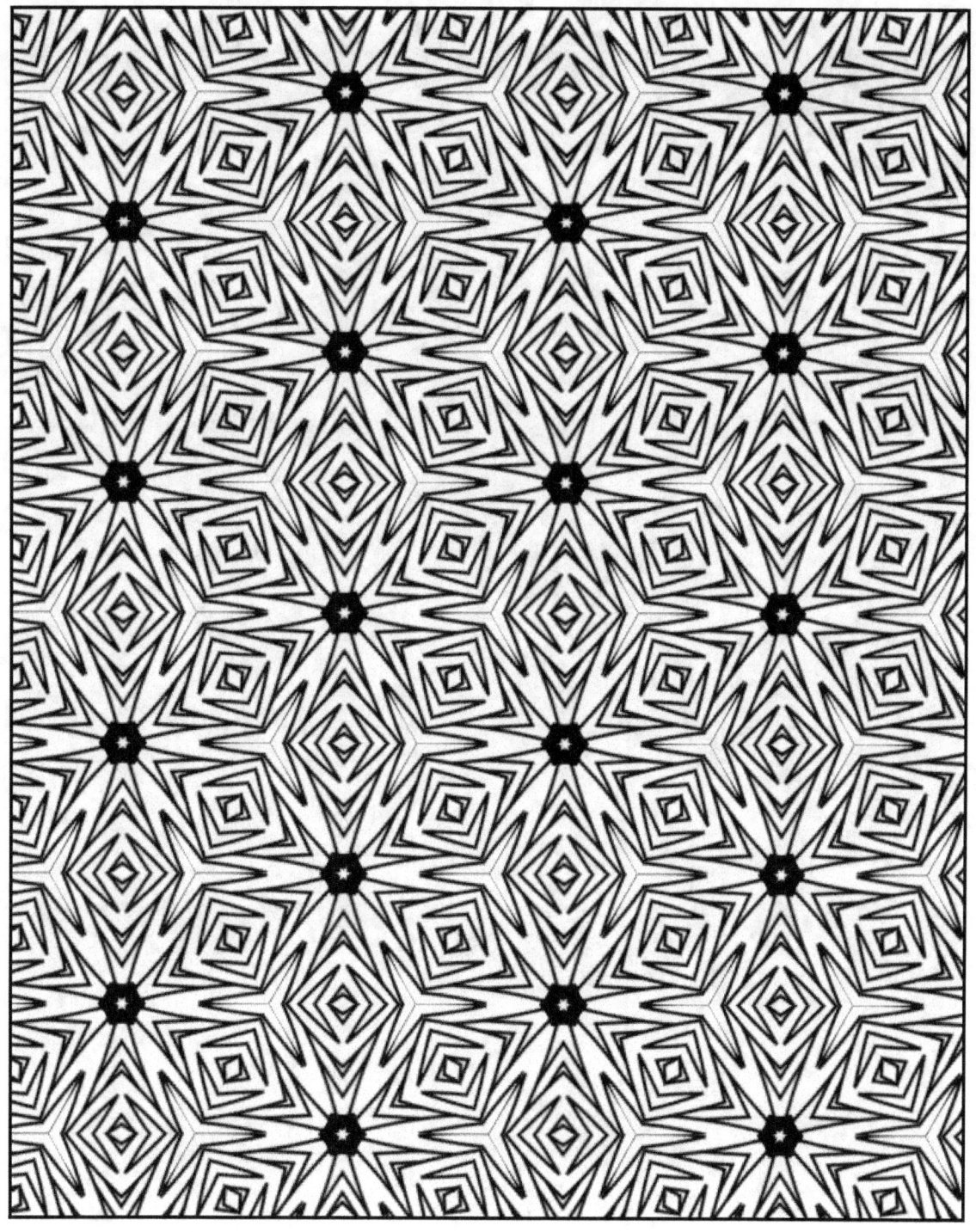

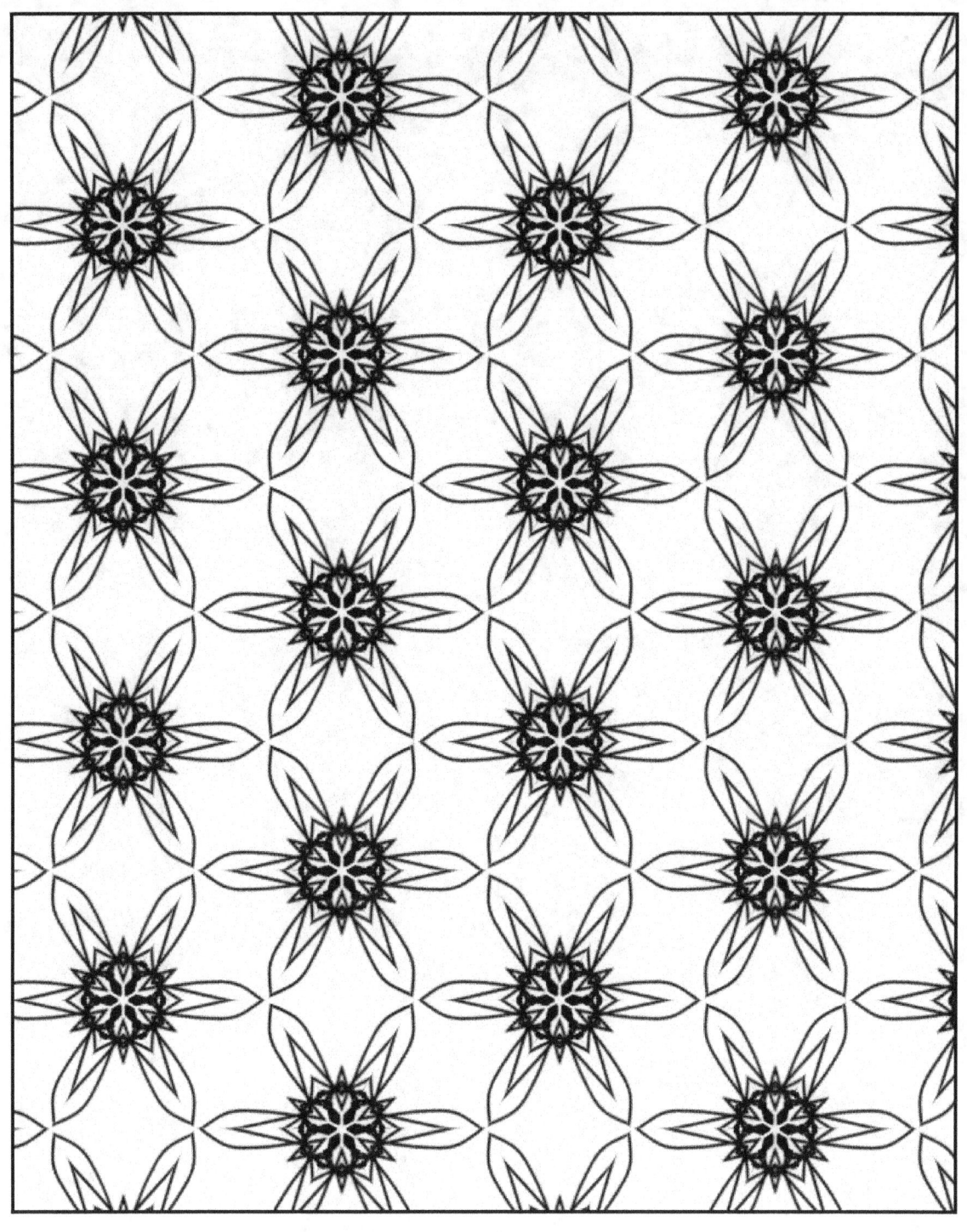

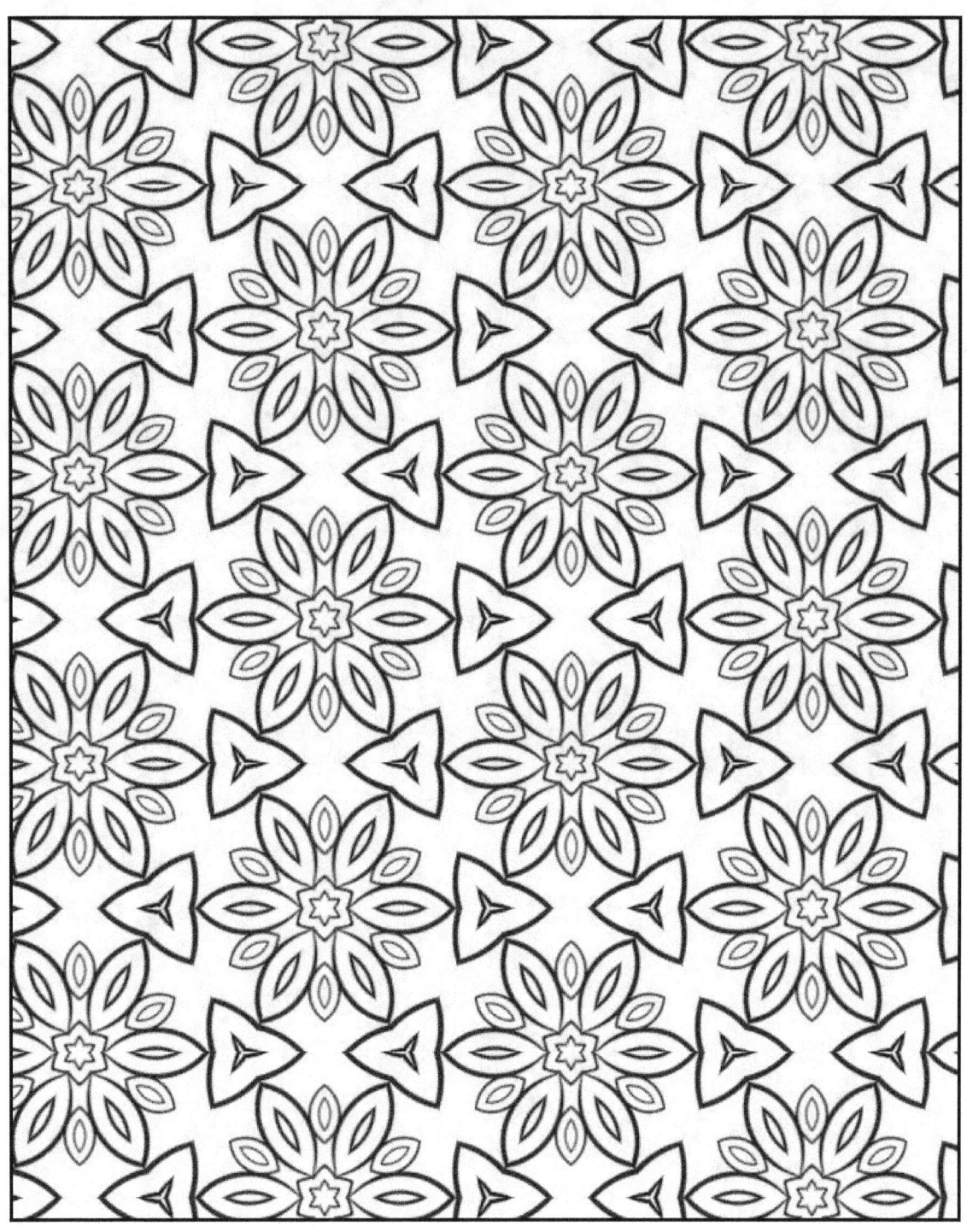

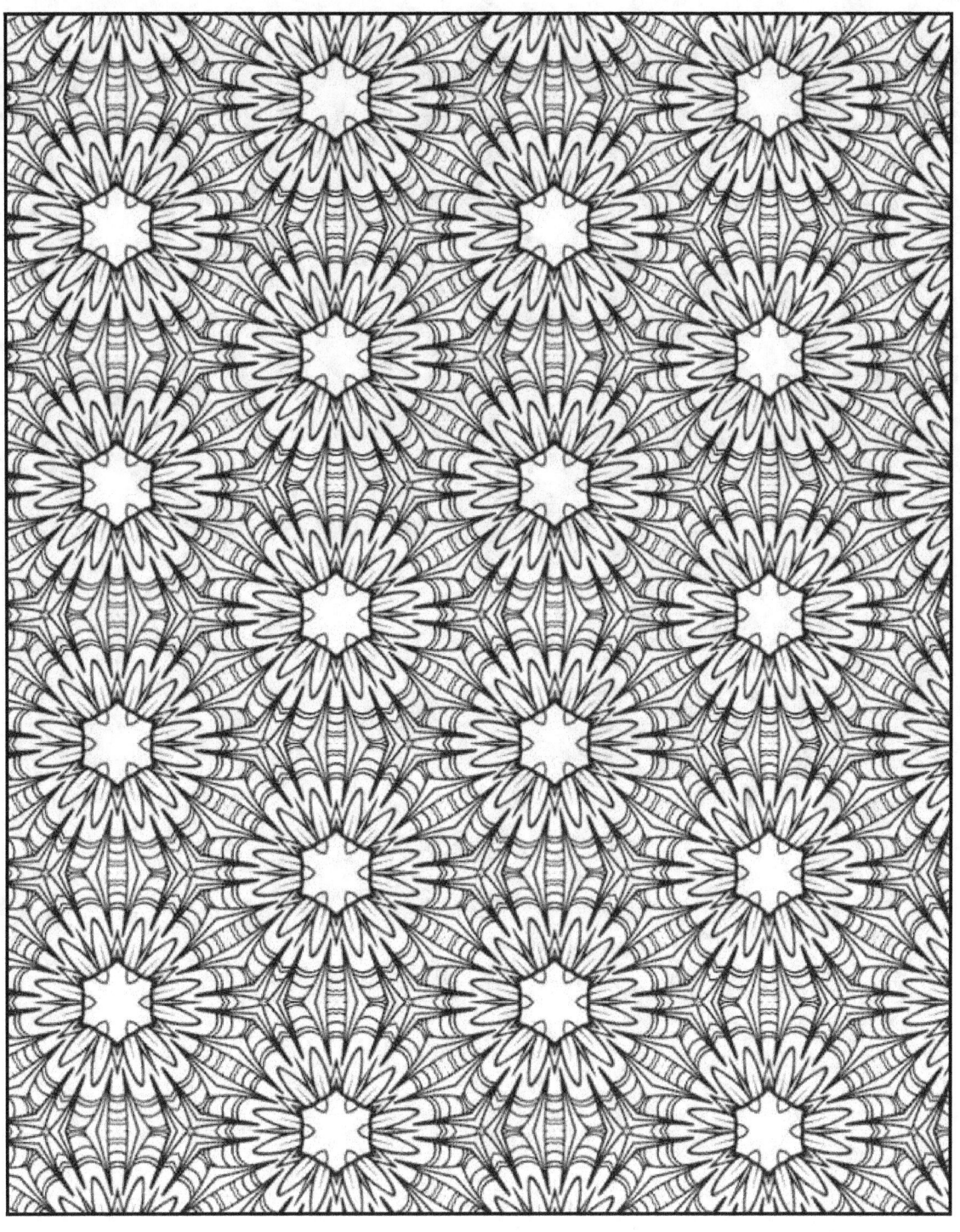

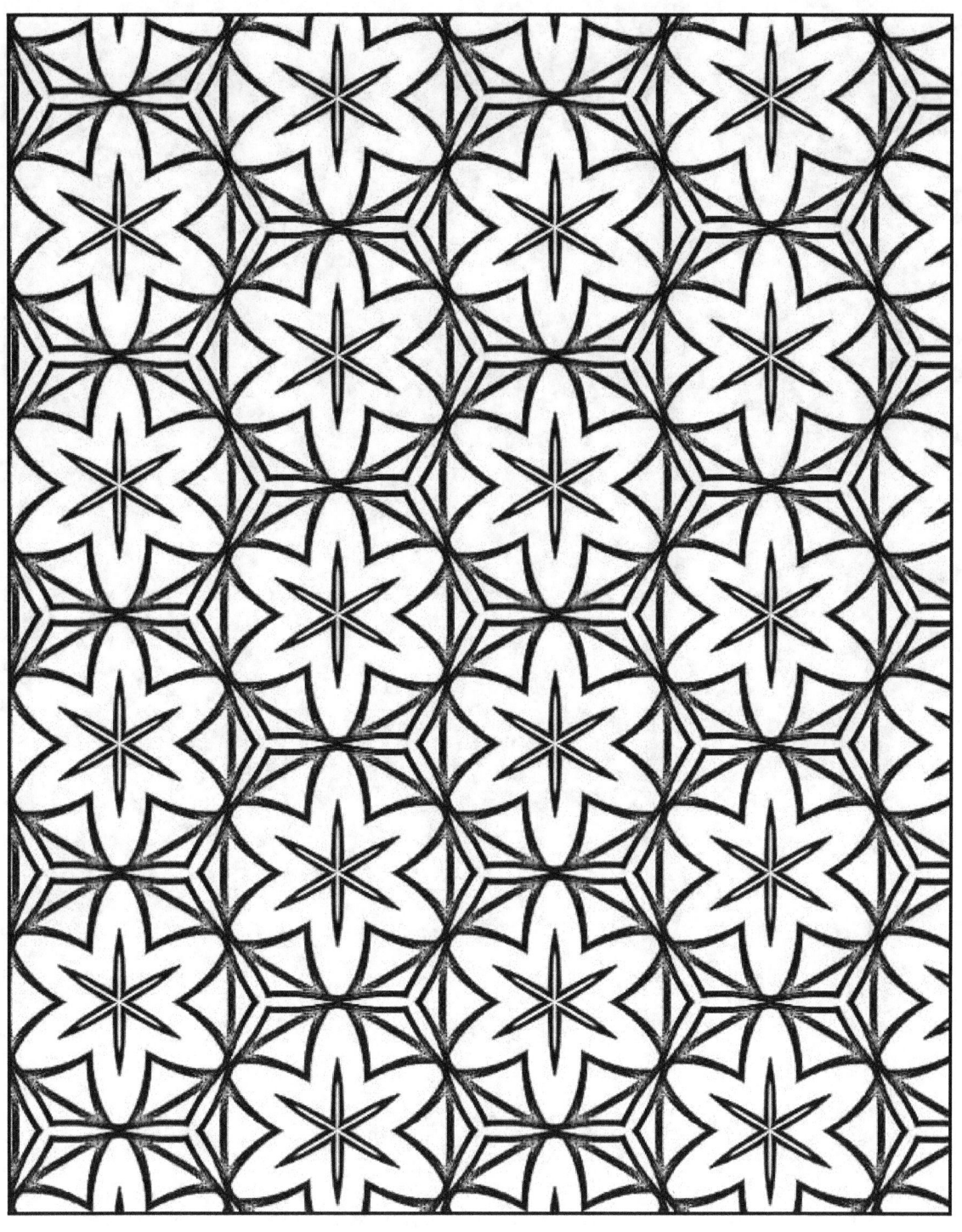

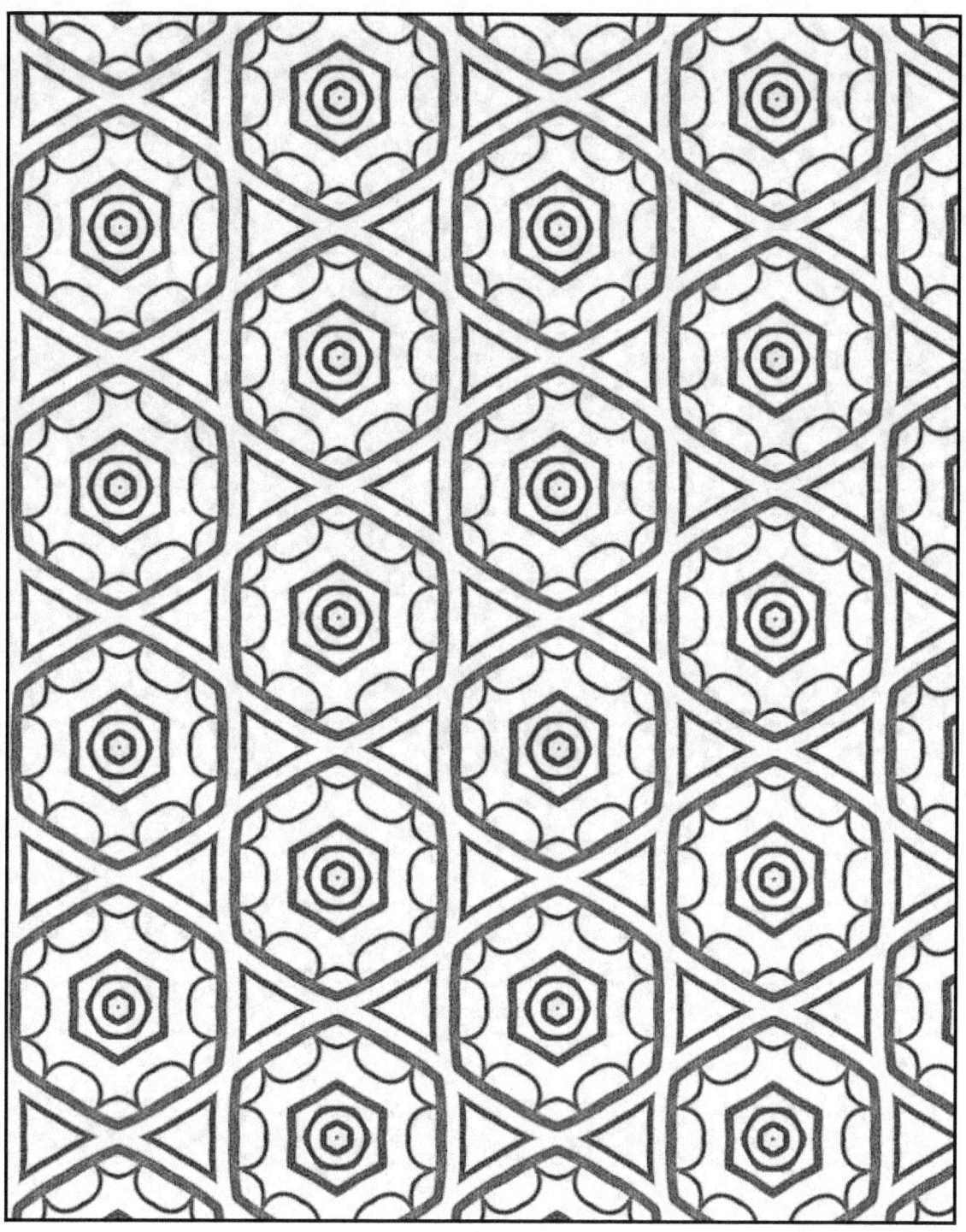

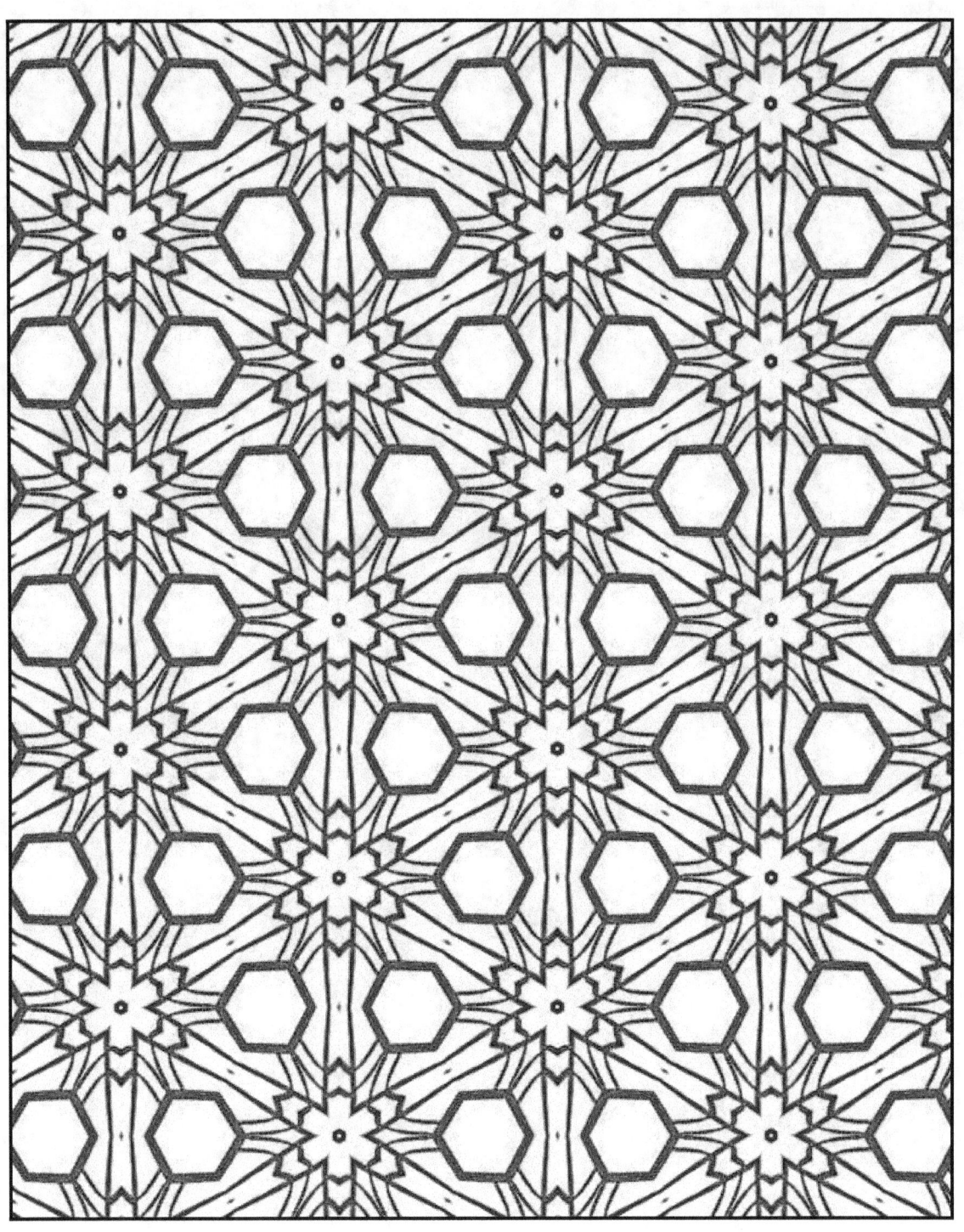

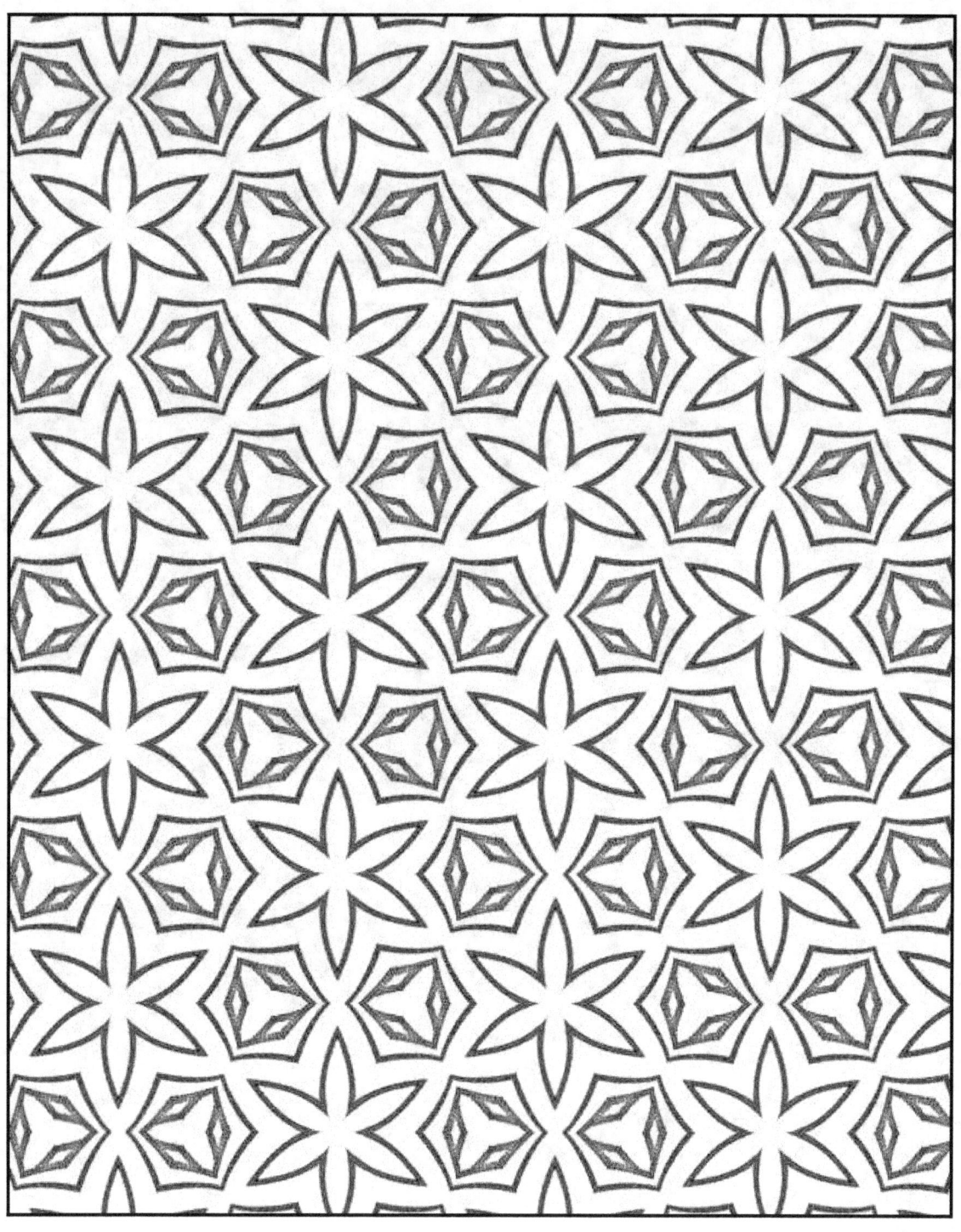

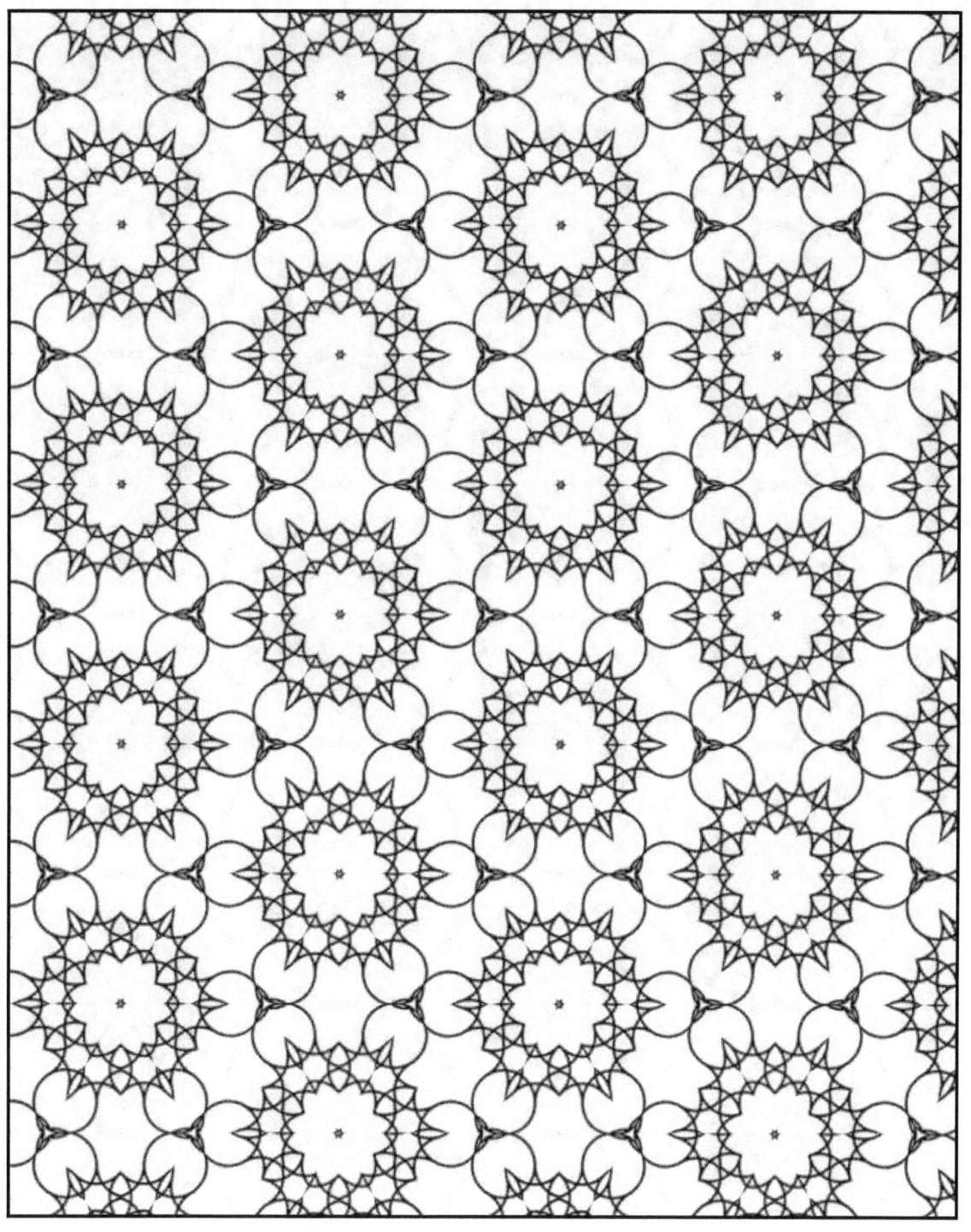

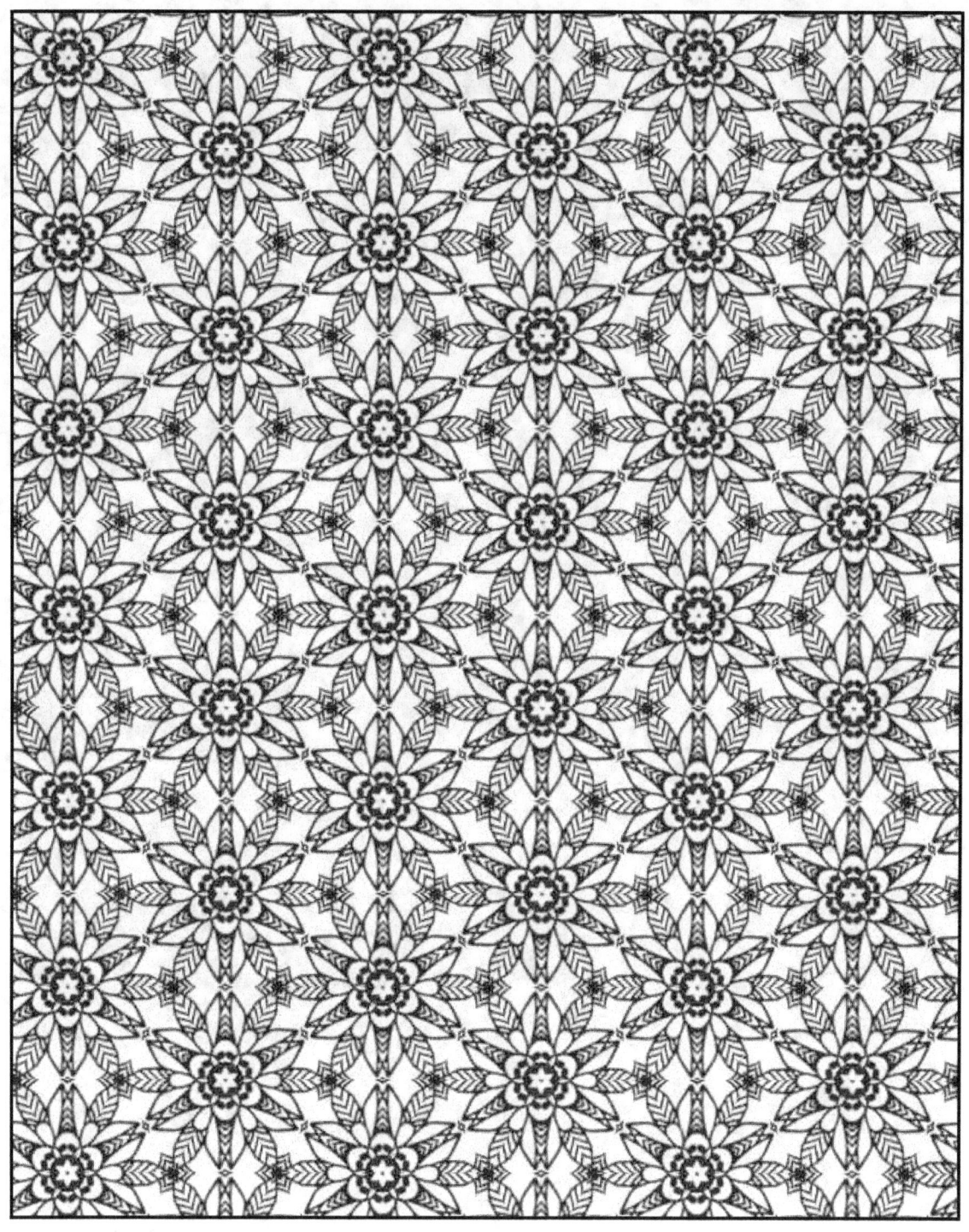

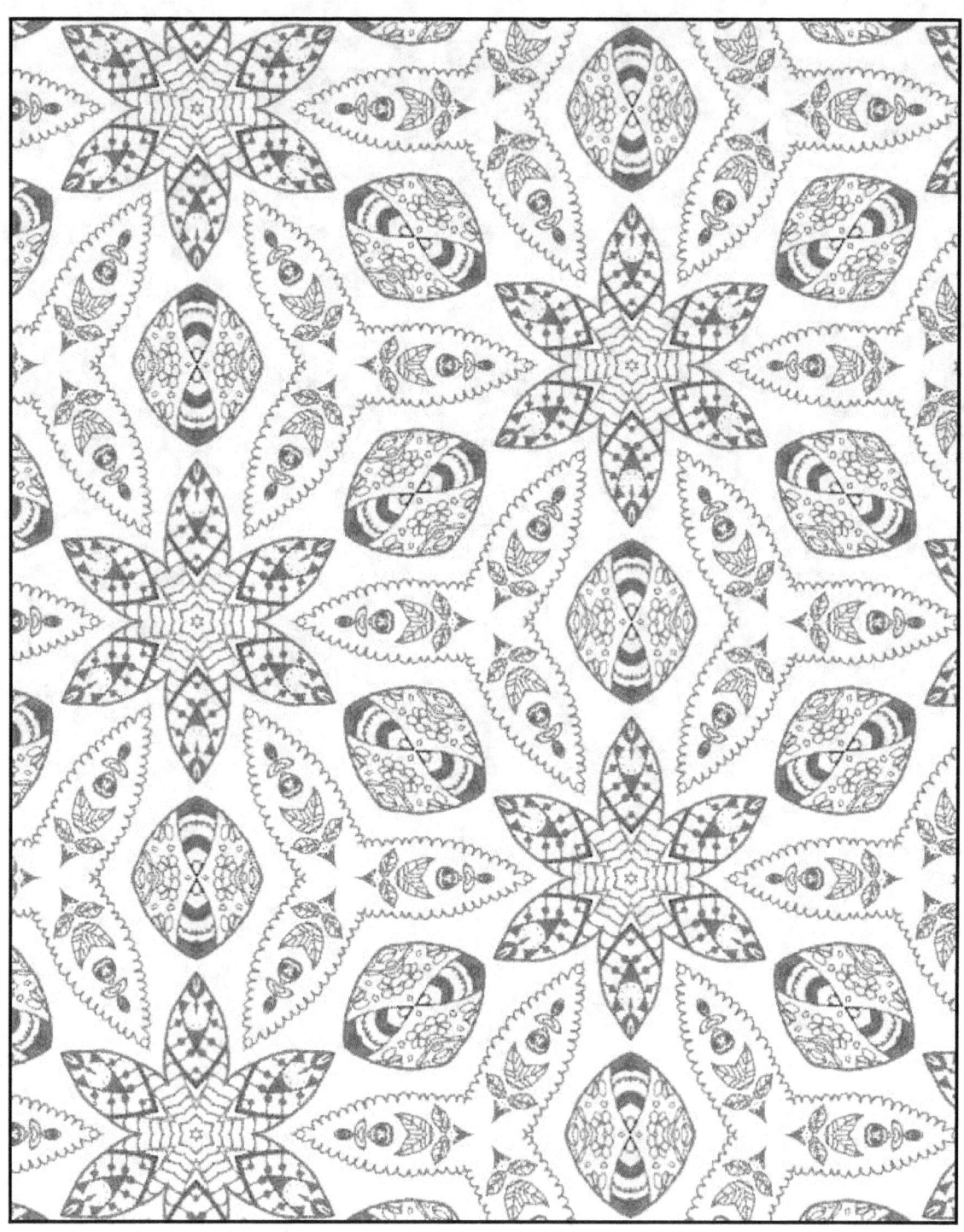

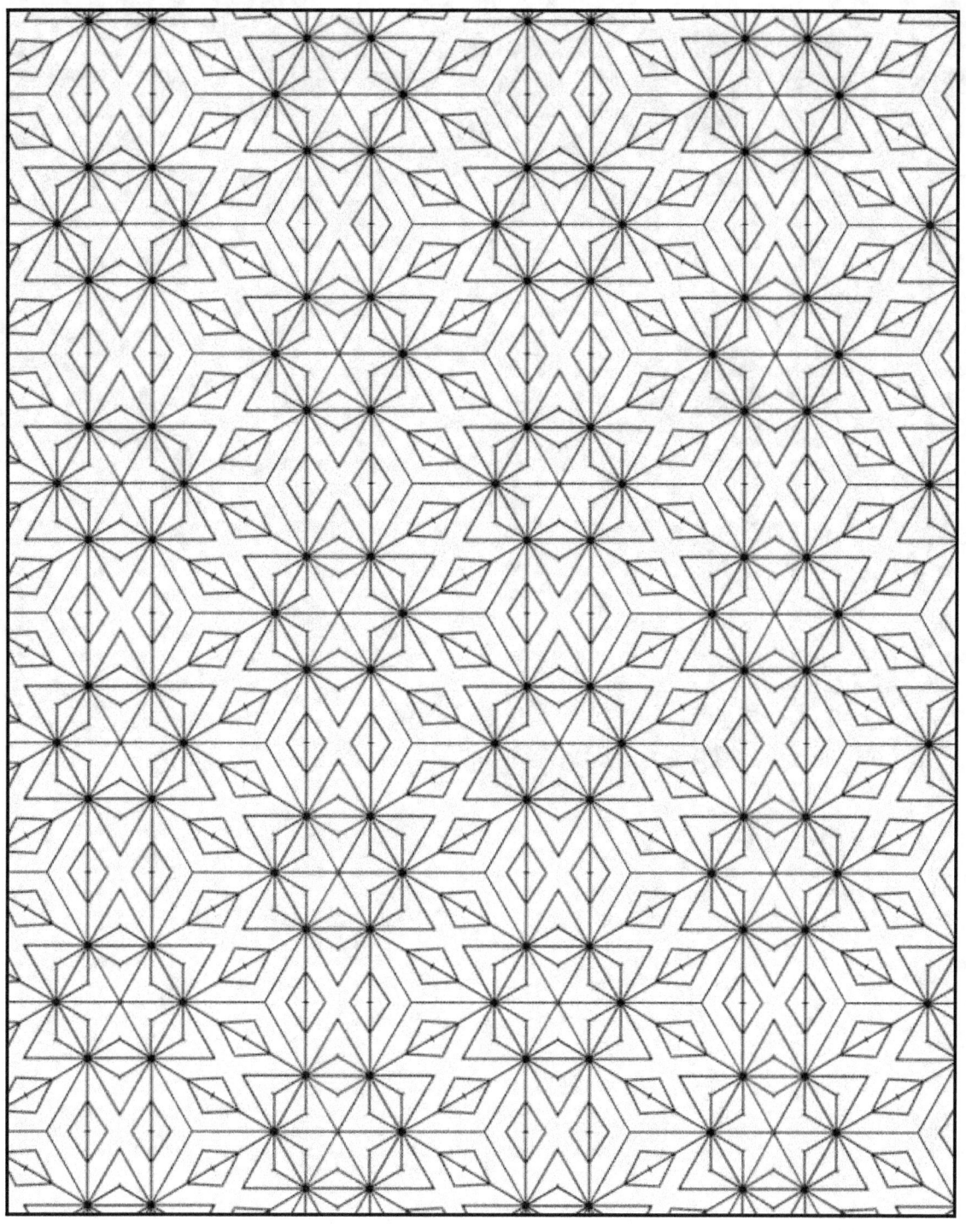

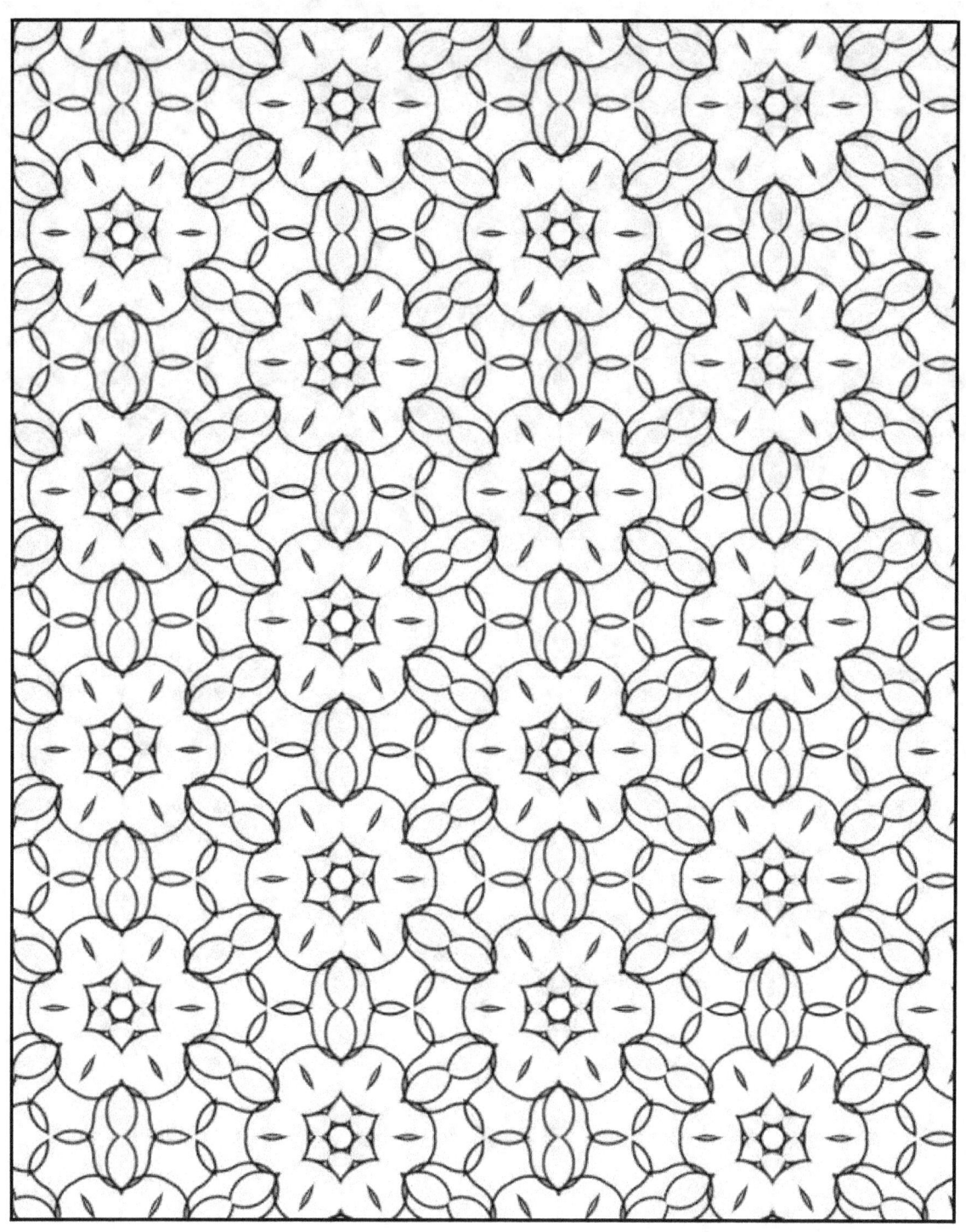

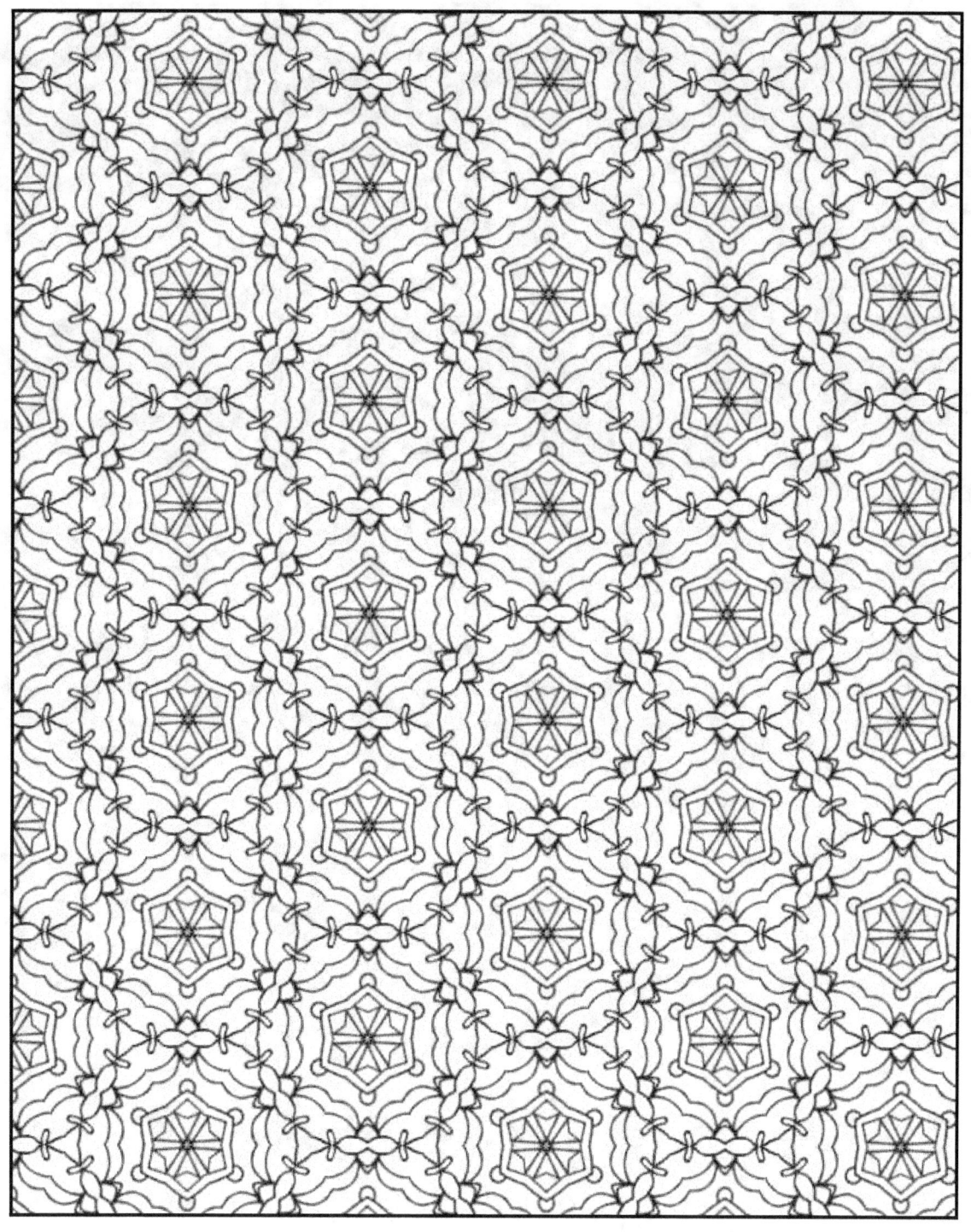

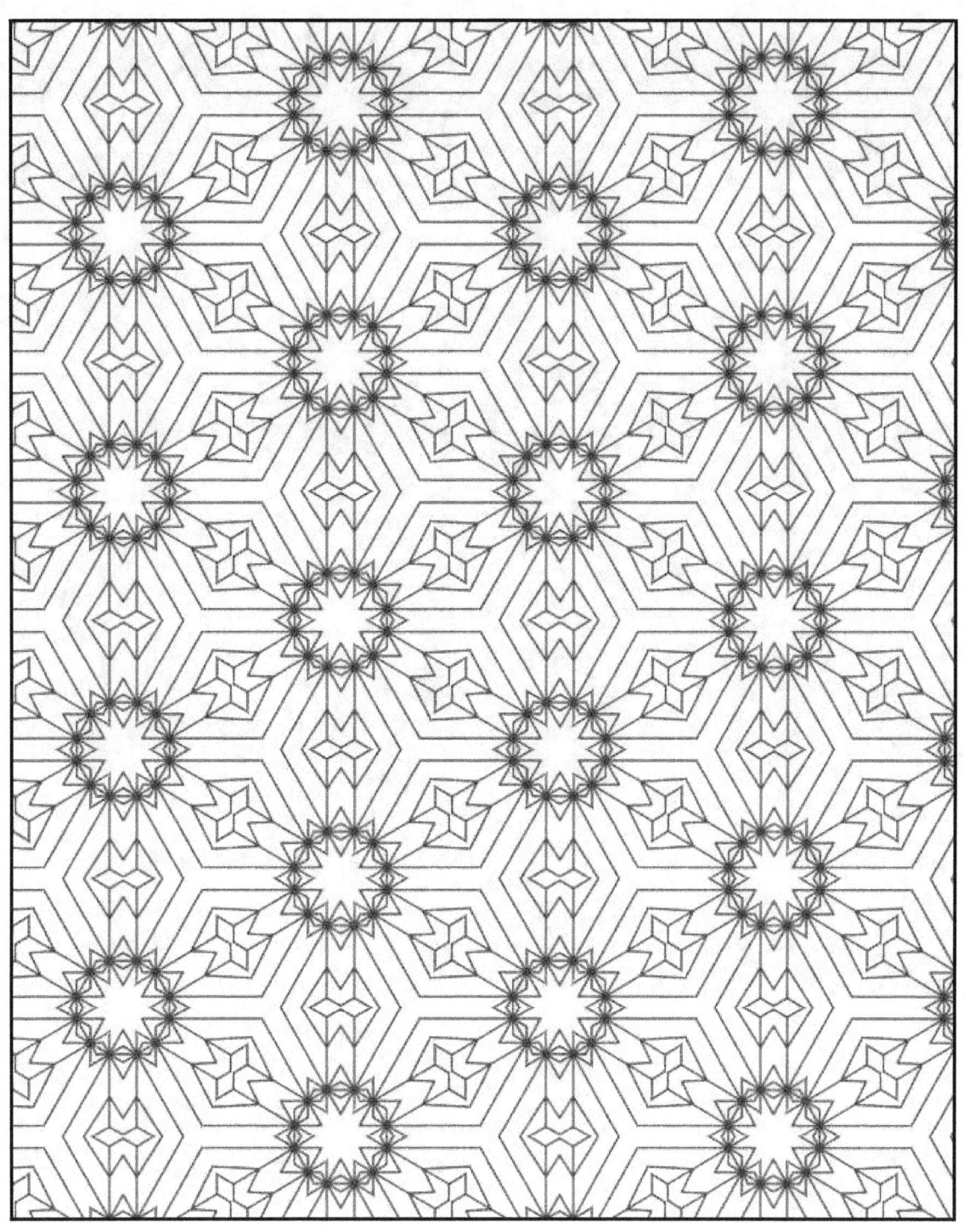

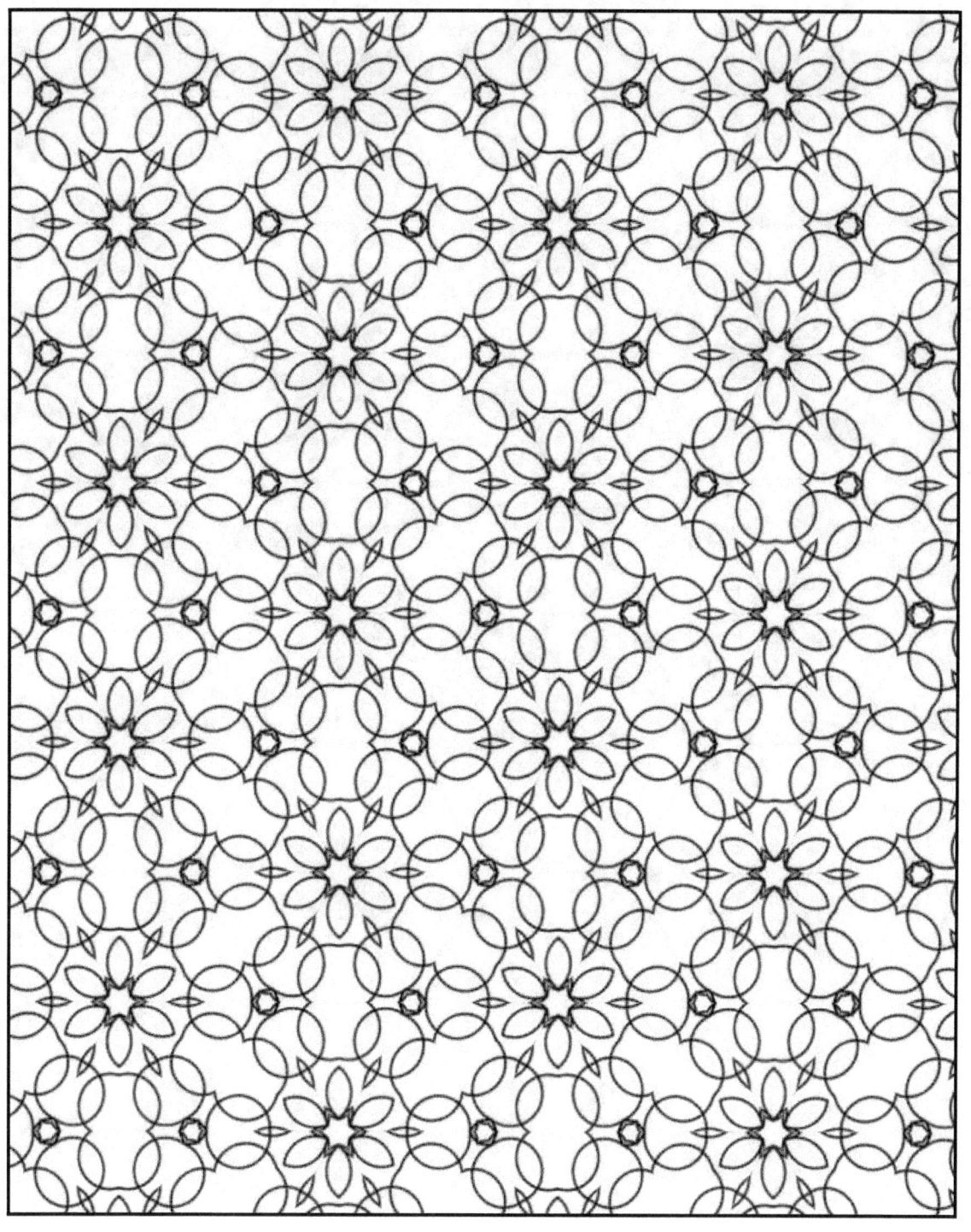

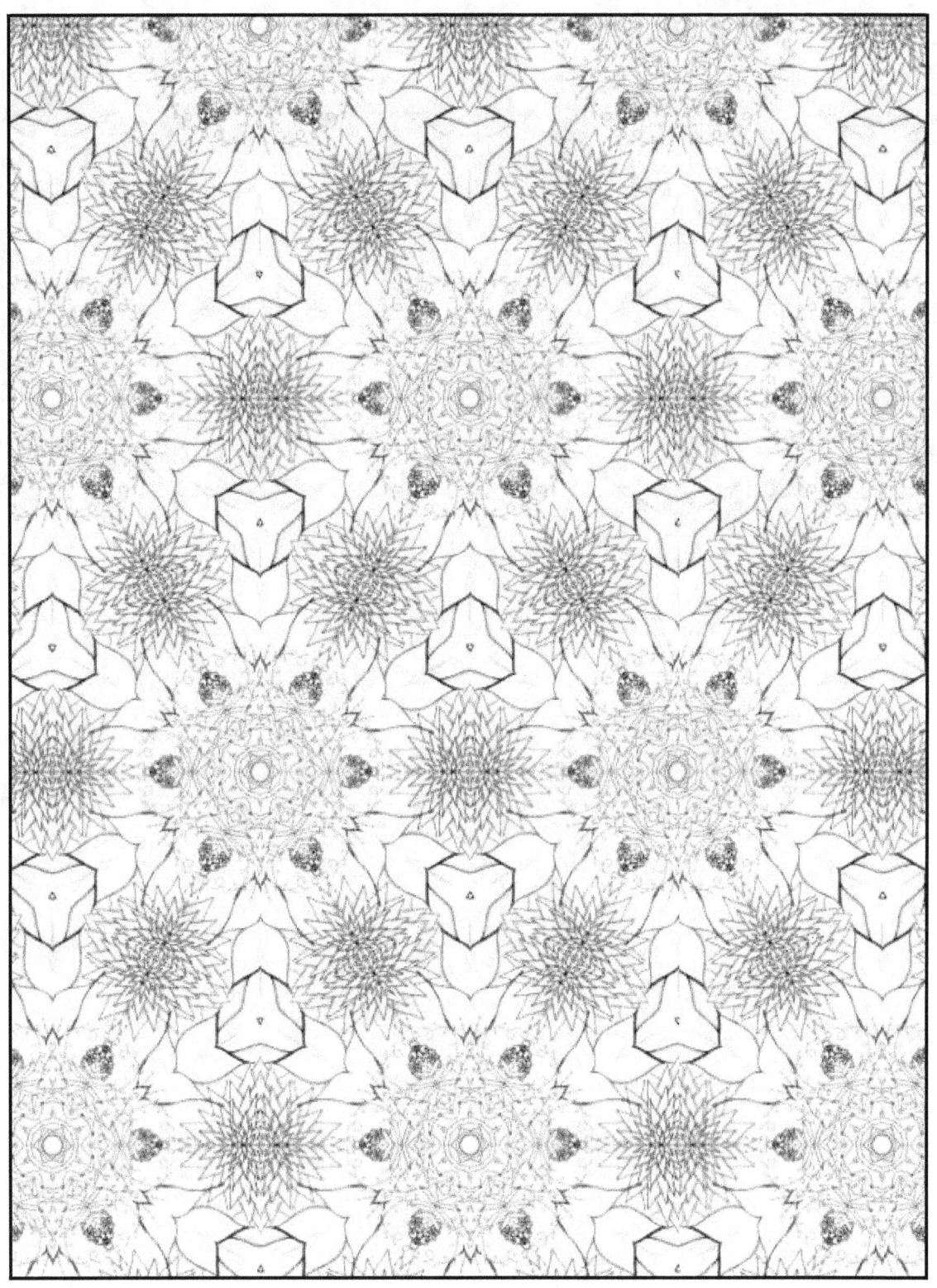

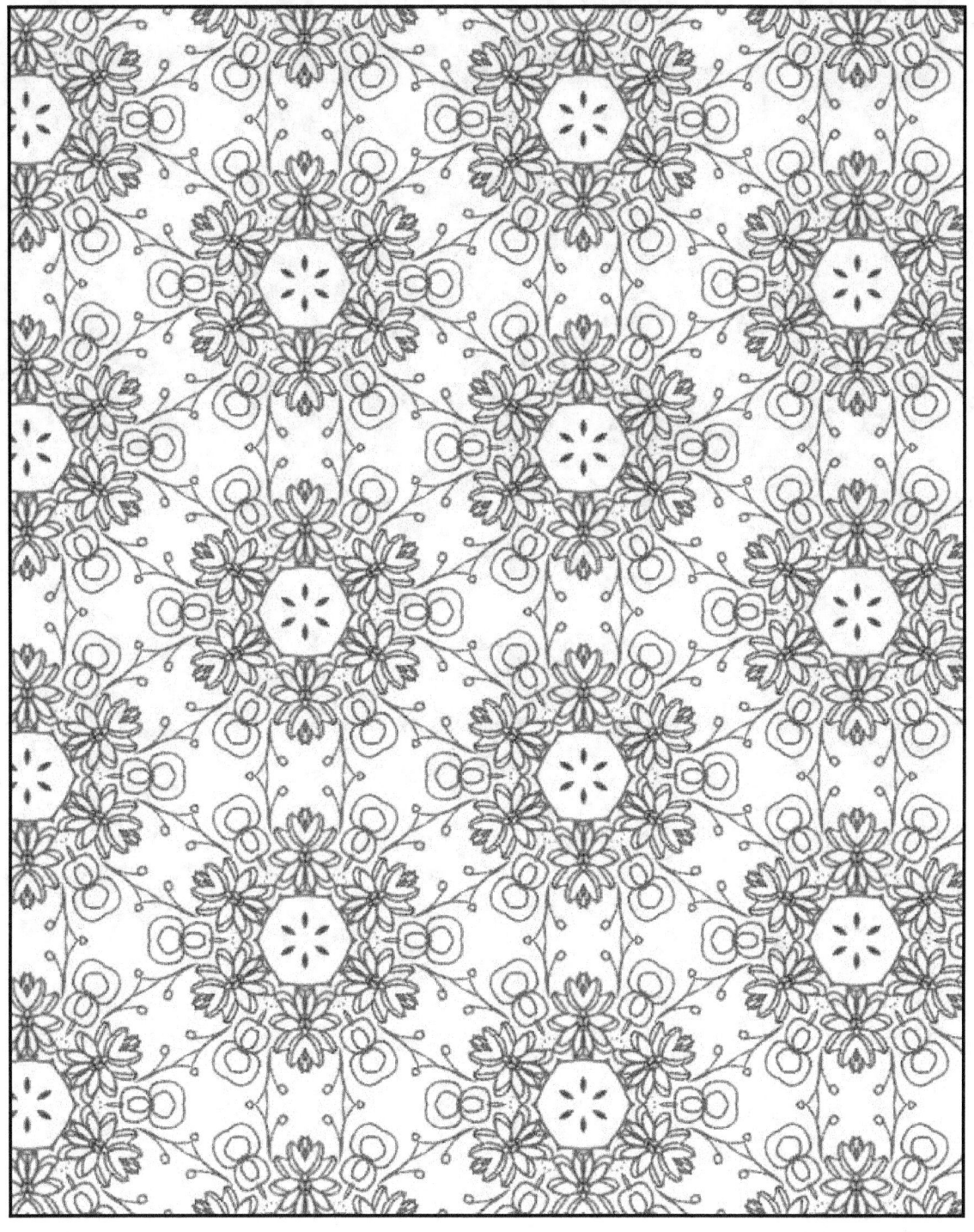

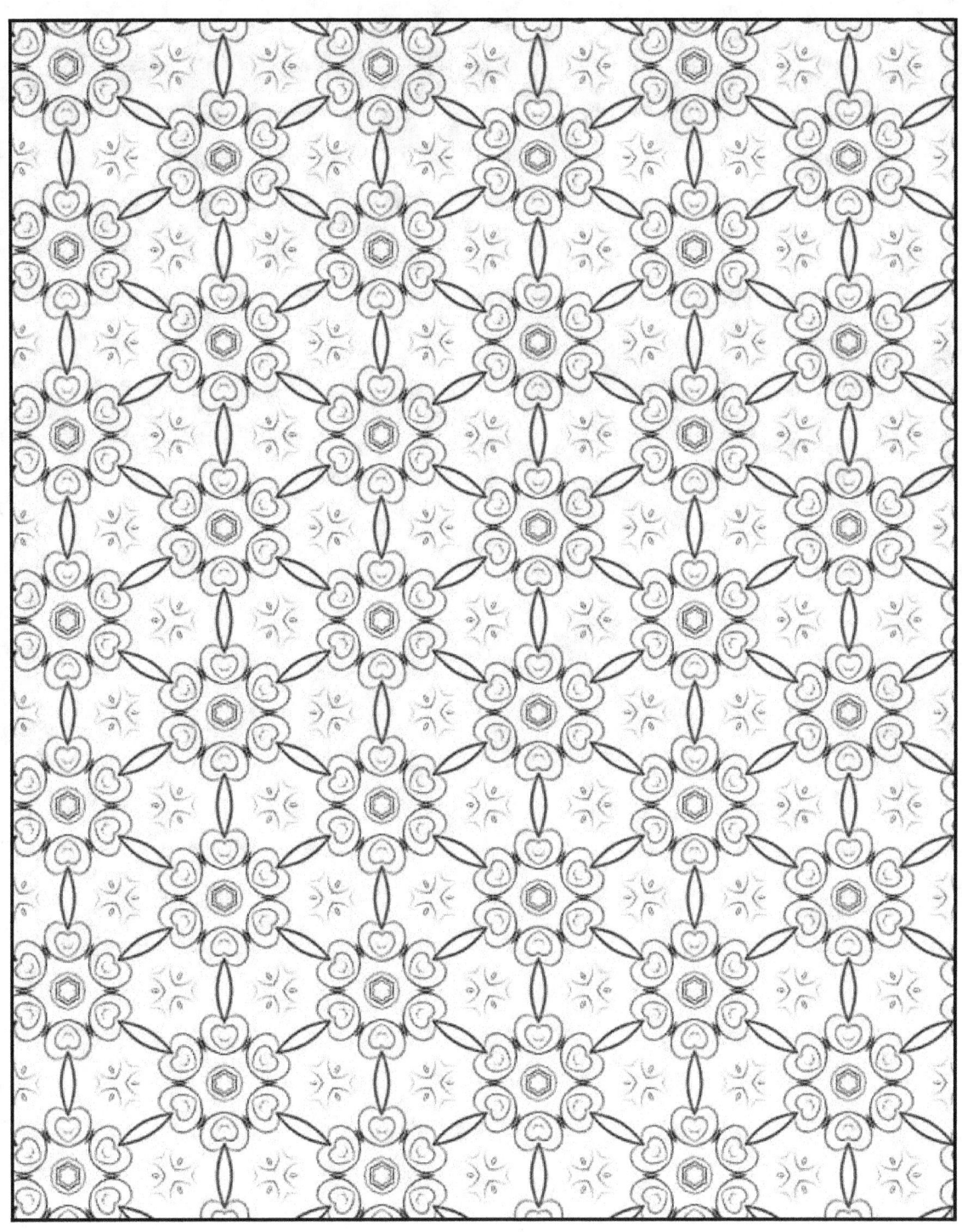

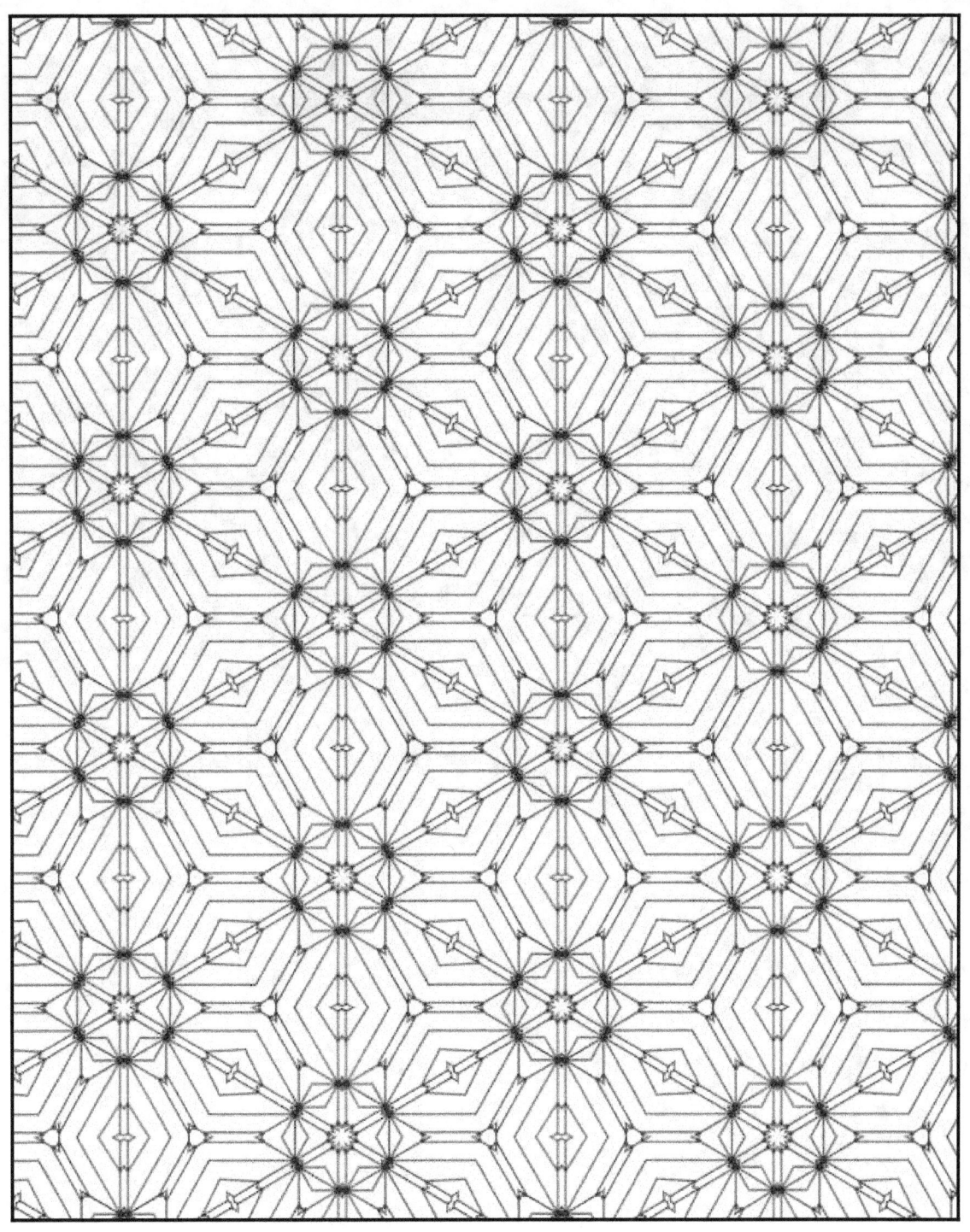

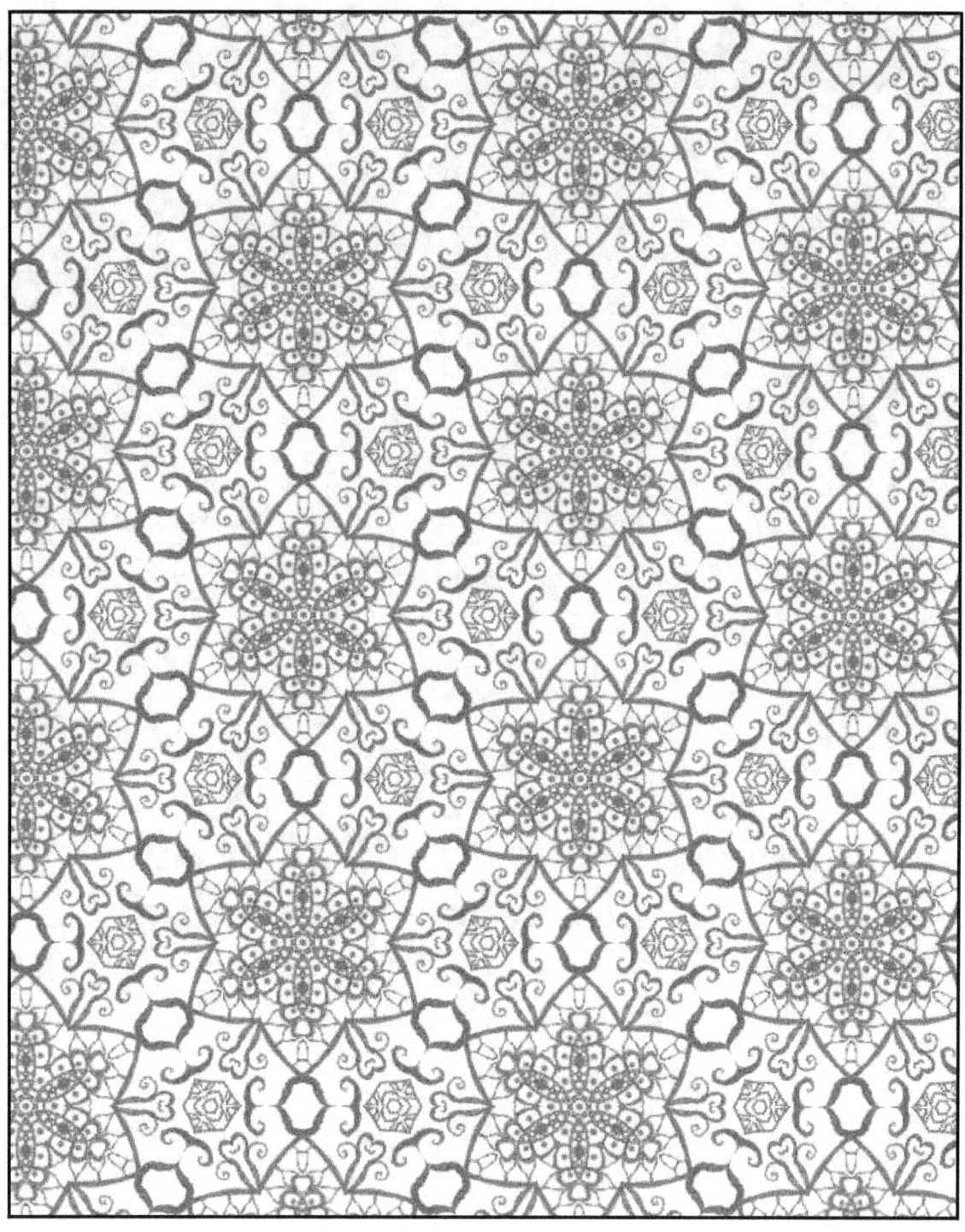

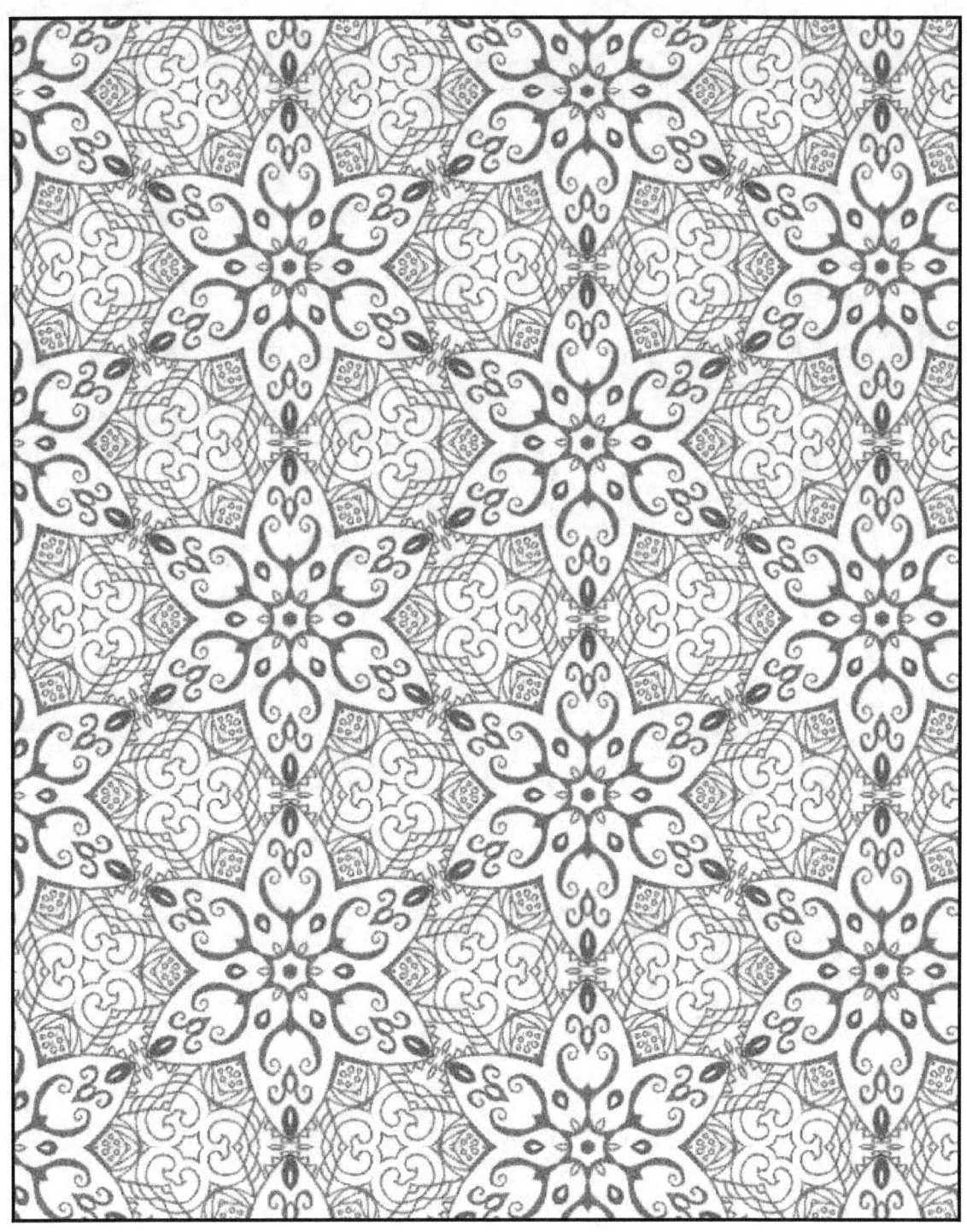

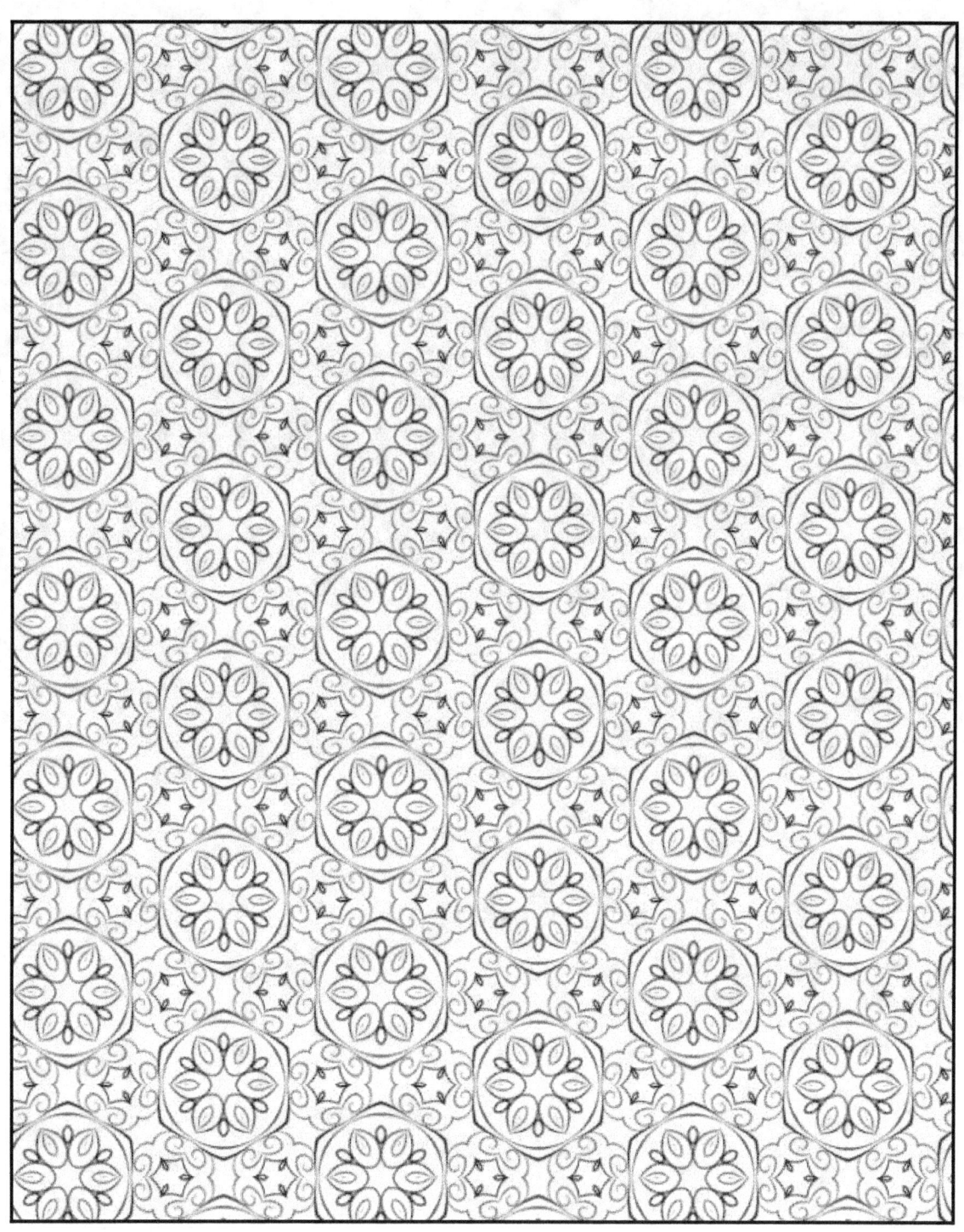

For More Books From Our

Publishing Company Including

Other Authors and Illustrators Visit

http://kdcoloring.com

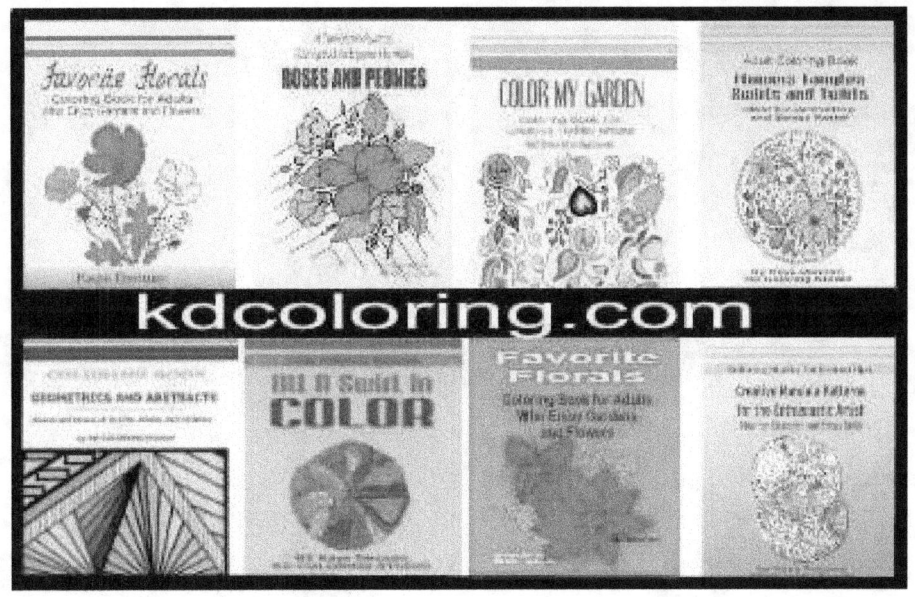